Water Resources Planning in New England

STUART G. ⌊KOCH⌋

⌈Water Resources Planning in New England⌋

∾∾∾

UNIVERSITY PRESS OF NEW ENGLAND

HANOVER, NEW HAMPSHIRE
LONDON, ENGLAND
1980

UNIVERSITY PRESS OF NEW ENGLAND
Sponsoring Institutions
Brandeis University
Clark University
Dartmouth College
University of New Hampshire
University of Rhode Island
Tufts University
University of Vermont

Library of Congress Catalog Card Number 79-66453
International Standard Book Number 0-87451-176-3
Printed in the United States of America

Library of Congress Cataloging in Publication data
will be found on the last printed page of this book.

Acknowledgments

This examination of the impact of citizen participation on bureaucratic accountability grew out of my involvement in a study of public participation in water resources planning, conducted at the Institute for Man and Environment (IME) of the University of Massachusetts. That project, supported in part by funds provided by the United States Department of the Interior, Office of Water Research and Technology, provided my data base.

I owe a debt of gratitude to the many people who have contributed to the book, especially my adviser, Lewis C. Mainzer, and Madge O. Ertel, the principal investigator of the IME project. Robert A. Shanley and Bernard B. Berger offered many suggestions, which have been incorporated below. David Harrison, manager of the Connecticut River Basin Program, made numerous substantive comments. Jenene Geerdes and William Northdurft, who were associated with the IME project, assisted in designing and conducting the survey.

Staff members of the New England River Basins Commission were extremely helpful, providing all information requested. Their contributions, as well as those of the citizen participants in the case studies, are greatly appreciated. Mildred Tubby typed the manuscript. Funds for typing and copying were provided by the Committee on Research of Vassar College.

Finally, I would like to add a special note of thanks to my grandmother, Viola M. George, to whom I dedicate this work.

Poughkeepsie, N.Y.   S. G. K.
March 1980

Contents

Tables

Abbreviations

BAC   Basin Advisory Committee
CAC   Citizens Advisory Committee
CAG   Citizens Advisory Group
CRC   Citizens Review Committee
CRBP   Connecticut River Basin Program
CZM   Coastal Zone Management
EPA   Environmental Protection Agency
FWPCA   Federal Water Pollution Control Act
LISS   Long Island Sound Study
NERBC   New England River Basins Commission
NEPA   National Environmental Policy Act
R/PAC   Research/Planning Advisory Committee
R/STF   Regional/Scientific Task Force
SAG   Science Advisory Group
SENE   Southeastern New England (Study)
SMT   Study Management Team

Water Resources Planning
in New England

Introduction

Public administrators play a major role in American policy-making; yet their involvement in such endeavors is not without cost. Recent studies have suggested that administrative policy-making poses certain potential hazards for a democratic society, since most bureaucratic officials are not directly subject to popular control through the electoral process. Nevertheless, authors have failed to agree on the precise nature of the problem or on ways to minimize the attendant dangers. By focusing on one increasingly important policy area, water resources, in one geographic setting, New England, this study explores the critical question "How can public bureaucrats, who may be motivated by a number of political, organizational, professional, and personal concerns, be held accountable in such a way as to enhance the chances of formulating responsible public policies?"[1] By using three case studies of water resources planning, one approach to this problem, increasing public participation, is assessed.

The literature of public administration has dealt with this concern for bureaucratic accountability in a variety of ways. For example, as seen in the classic debate between Carl Friedrich and Herman Finer, writers have argued for increased control over federal administrators by the President, the Congress, the courts, fellow professionals, or the public at large. Authors like Kaufman and Powell have developed overviews of these different approaches to controlling bureaucracy, and in so doing have helped to clarify the compatibility of, or the tensions between, various means of holding bureaucrats accountable.[2] Still others, including Gittell, have evaluated for given agencies or policy areas both the application of one of the above approaches and the techniques to implement them.[3] Finally, Pitkin and others, discussing what it means to be accountable or representative, have aided in the understanding of complex political concepts.[4]

In part, the literature suggests that the meaning of "accountability," like that of related concepts—for example, representation—is imprecise. To say that administrative officials in a democratic society should be accountable is, generally speaking, to say that they should be answerable legally and/or politically for the discharge of their duties. As Pitkin observes, however, traditional concerns for accountability have offered few insights into how administrators ought to act in policy-making and related activities.[5] Similarly, there has been relatively little assessment of how various means of assuring accountability might improve administrative policy-making performance.

Starting from this point, one can identify several basic needs for further research on the subject of administrative accountability. First, there is a need to understand better the role that bureaucrats play in the formulation of public policies. Second, there is a need to determine the impact of efforts to increase accountability on bureaucratic behavior and on the policy outputs and outcomes that result. Third, further case studies are necessary in order to evaluate the application of given approaches to accountability, especially in policy areas that have not yet been adequately examined. Fourth, where certain approaches seem useful, there is the need to evaluate specific techniques for holding administrators accountable.

The present study addresses itself to these needs. The core of the research is an analysis of public participation in three regional planning studies conducted by the New England River Basins Commission (NERBC), an agency charged with coordinating federal, state, and interstate plans for the management of water and related land resources in its region. By analyzing citizen involvement in the NERBC's Long Island Sound Study, Southeastern New England Study, and Connecticut River Basin Supplemental

Study, I examine two hypotheses: (1) that broadened public participation improves the quality of public policies, and (2) that participation in administrative decision-making enhances the democratic nature of American government.

The approach has limitations. My analysis focuses primarily on public participation in *planning* activities, rather than in subsequent *policy-making* stages. Also, I do not consider all possible impacts of citizen involvement, such as its effects on the individual self-development of those participating. But I can and do study in detail one particular concern meriting attention, knowing that other concerns beyond the purview of this book exist. By focusing on a specific policy area, water resources, I can consider the applicability both of the concept of citizen participation and of specific techniques for involving the public in this policy area.

CHAPTER ONE

Problems in
Water Resources Planning

Public administrators in the United States create as well as execute public policies and programs. As the scope of national public policies has expanded dramatically in the United States in recent decades, so has the role of public administrators in defining such policies. The many dimensions of this role reflect the fact that public policies are formed in a variety of ways. For example, they may be formally enunciated in statutes or agency rules and guidelines, or they may develop over time in a less deliberate manner, as the sum of individual decisions by governmental officials.[1] Indeed, policies may be unannounced, unrecognized, or unintended.[2] Therefore, administrative involvement in the creation of public policy necessarily occurs at a variety of junctures.

Public Policy-Making by Bureaucracy

Bureaucrats create public policy by participating in the law-making process. They initiate budget requests, propose bills, testify at hearings, give informal advice, and perform long-term planning and policy analysis. Administrators in regulatory agencies also use rule-making powers to clarify vague Congressional mandates. When the Interstate Commerce Commission determines "just and reasonable rates" for the railroads, it shapes national transportation policy.[3] Such policies are further defined through the adjudicative mechanisms within the same agencies. In addition, bureaucrats routinely create policy as they establish administrative guidelines, thereby setting forth additional criteria for the distribution of benefits and services, as well as procedures for handling individual cases. Finally, administrators choose among alternatives, determining "how the power of the state should be used in specific cases."[4] Taken collectively, these latter decisions constitute public policy.

In practice these different dimensions of policy-making are highly interrelated. Decisions made and lessons learned in implementation will be later reflected in proposals for legislation. Where the direction of laws ends and bureaucratic discretion begins is difficult to determine. Public policy-making is in fact a continuous process in which policies are being formulated—both implicitly and explicitly—as they are being administered.[5]

The specialized knowledge and the political power of administrators have also increased their involvement in the formulation of public policies. Bureaucrats are sources of knowledge rarely equaled elsewhere in government. This may reflect their particular education or training (expertise), but frequently stems simply from the extensive division of labor in most agencies and their closeness to the implementation of ongoing policies.[6] Moreover, despite the reluctance of administrators to acknowledge their political activities, they frequently engage in lobbying and public relations efforts.[7] To promote their views, administrators cultivate the support of clientele and other groups with which they share policy concerns. Despite the variances in such support, it has been an important source of bureaucratic power—although the price of such alliances is to accept the views of constituents as a major influence on agency decisions.

In summary, bureaucrats play a varied and influential, if not dominant, role in public policy-making, a role enhanced by their expertise, their political strength, and the inseparability of administrative and policy-making functions. These factors suggest that administrators will continue to influence American public policy in the foreseeable future. As Norman Thomas observes: "It is doubtful that any modern industrial society could manage the daily operation of its public affairs without bureaucratic organizations in which officials play a major policy-making role."[8]

Bureaucratic Accountability and Democracy

This increased involvement by bureaucrats in public policy-making poses potentially serious problems for American democracy. A basic criterion of democratic government is that public officials, as representatives of the people, should be "accountable" for their actions—that is, answerable both legally and politically to the citizenry for the performance of their duties.[9] However, the vast majority of public administrators, who are hired rather than elected or appointed, are several steps removed from direct public control.[10] Elections, for example, provide a direct though infrequent mechanism for holding congressmen and presidents answerable, but bureaucrats are far less subject to their pressures. Even though bureaucratic policy-making may exhibit a trustee dimension, a general commitment to serve the interests of the public, there is little direct accountability involved.[11] Thus, as administrators have increasingly become authors of public policy, governmental accountability has diminished.[12]

This expression of concern is not intended as an indictment of either bureaucracy or individual bureaucrats.[13] It stems less from a fear that individuals will deliberately abuse their power than from a recognition that bureaucratic policy-making, which is not subject to electoral controls, is a highly complex process in which a variety of political, organizational, professional, and human factors intervene.

Intervening political factors. Because bureaucrats operate in a highly politicized arena, demands are constantly thrust upon them, and deals are struck. Indeed, the adoption of a given rule or standard depends as much on its base of political support as on its intrinsic merits.[14] Thus, as administrators interact with interest groups, key Congressmen, executive officials, and one another, policy develops as a series of compromises which reflect, according to Graham Allison, "the pulling and hauling that is politics."[15] As critics of interest-group theory point out, however, such compromises may represent only the interests of major political actors and not necessarily those of the general public.

Intervening organizational factors. Various organizational characteristics and concerns also limit the ability of administrators to define and act in the interests of the public. First, as Francis Rourke observes: "The inequality of power inherent in hierarchy means that the views of highly placed individuals carry immense weight, not because of the persuasiveness of their arguments but simply because of the exalted status from which they speak."[16] Second, the fact that bureaucratic decision-making is often closed to the public makes it difficult for all interested parties to participate and obscures the real sources of influence on decisions.[17] Third, concerns for an organization's survival or betterment, as well as for the public welfare, frequently weigh on the minds of administrators and color their perceptions of reality. In the extreme, such pressures may cause administrators to avoid innovative policies that might alter the *status quo*.[18]

Intervening professional factors. In addition, because professional groups have come to dominate many agencies, or at least their subunits, resulting policies tend to reflect the standards and values of these groups. Each of these professions, observes Frederick Mosher,

> brings to an organization its own particularized view of the world and of the agency's role and mission in it. The perspective and motivation of each professional are shaped at least to some extent by the lens provided him by his professional education, by his prior professional experiences, and by his professional colleagues.[19]

The goals and strategies embraced by professional groups represent, however, the culmination of debate within a select, homogeneous group with a particular orientation and, hence, the values of only one segment of society.[20] Moreover, professionals are likely to focus primarily on the substance of work and neglect broader value questions.[21]

Intervening personal factors. Finally, personal factors, too, may affect administrative policy-making. In Allison's words: "each person comes to his position with baggage in tow, including sensitivity to certain issues, commitments to various programs, and personal standing and debts with groups in the society."[22] Because the background characteristics of bureaucrats imperfectly mirror those of the citizenry as a whole, however, their sensitivities, commitments, and debts may not be widely shared.[23] Personal concerns about one's career also make it difficult for an administrator to support policies that are potentially good but might jeopardize his job.

Although the influence of these different factors varies from case to case and certainly requires further study, their impact, both individually and collectively, is a cause for genuine concern. The pressures upon administrators to serve only segments of the public, their agency, their profession, or themselves, rather than the public at large, are real. Their existence underscores the need for enhancing the accountability of public administrators.

Bureaucratic Accountability and Responsible Public Policy

Alarmed by the trend toward increased bureaucratic power, many authors have sought methods of preventing administrators from overstepping their proper authority. In an era when bureaucratic policy-making has expanded tremendously, however, such approaches, though important, are no longer adequate. They show scant regard for the quality of the public policies which administrators help to produce on a day-to-day basis. A more policy-oriented, less legalistic approach to administrative accountability is required, one aimed at motivating bureaucratic officials to use their power to serve the interests of the citizenry. The critical question is: "How can public administrators be held accountable, so that they will create responsible public policies?"

Standards for judging performance must be established. This is a difficult task, for criteria do not submit to a logical formulation.[24] Authors who have addressed this problem have disagreed on specific criteria.[25] Yet the notions of "responsibility" and "responsible" provide a flexible series of standards by which policies can be evaluated.[26] The terms can be broken into three categories. To say that a public policy is "responsible" is to say that it is lawful, that it is responsive, and that it is effective.

(1) *Lawfulness*: A policy that is lawful is consistent with the rule of law and due process. Public policies may be evaluated in terms of how well they adhere to existing laws and regulations, as well as to the Constitution itself. Also, the concern for individual rights in the Constitution requires that policies provide procedural safe-

guards to guarantee that decisions will be "predictable, under-standable, and equitable."[27]

(2) *Responsiveness*: Because American public policy is formu-lated in a democratic setting, it should also be judged by the way it responds to public needs and preferences. Traditionally, the major test of responsiveness has been how well policies reflect the prefer-ences of the people at large, or their designated representatives.[28] Public needs must also be taken into account, however, since pub-lic preferences may not be formulated, may not be clear, or may be based on misperceptions of the situation.[29]

(3) *Effectiveness*: Given the limited resources available to gov-ernment, one may evaluate public policies on the basis of their mean-end effectiveness.[30] Is a given policy more likely than alterna-tive policies to bring about desired outcomes? "Effectiveness" in this sense is close in meaning to "efficiency," provided that the usage of the latter encompasses social and political as well as eco-nomic costs.[31]

These criteria focus on a broad range of concerns, which are not always compatible.[32] What is efficient may not accord with public preference or procedural safeguards. For example, the suggestion by a federal agency to reduce parking spaces and increase fees in cities in order to reduce automobile traffic and thus pollution might be effective if implemented, but proves unacceptable to the public. It is impossible to isolate a single responsible public policy for a given situation, for a number of alternatives always exist. I suggest, however, that to the extent that one or more of these cri-teria are ignored, the interests of the general public will suffer. The very complexity of the criteria increases the likelihood that they will not be given full consideration by bureaucratic officials, and emphasizes the need for supervision to make sure that they are.

The Role of Bureaucrats

These trends and problems assume their own particular dynam-ics in different policy areas, such as water resources. Indeed, water resources planning is a complex policy-making process in which administrative officials play a clearly predominant role in identify-ing water-related problems and in developing and evaluating alternative strategies for solving them.[33] Typically, water resources planning is undertaken in the form of multi-year studies or investigations by one or more agencies, although such efforts vary tremendously in geographical scope and the number of problems examined. A study may focus on the problems of a given community or those of an entire river basin or region. It may deal with a specific water-related concern, such as flood control or water quality, or encompass multiple problems. In any case, the final products are usually detailed planning reports, which serve as the basis for further policy-making activities, including the authorization and funding of given water projects.

At the federal level alone, the list of agencies involved in water resources planning is seemingly endless. It includes the Army Corps of Engineers, the Bureau of Reclamation, the Soil Conservation Service, the National Weather Service, the Federal Energy Regulatory Commission, the Fish and Wildlife Service, the Heritage Conservation and Recreation Service, the Environmental Protection Agency, and the Department of Housing and Urban Development. The Tennessee Valley Authority, federal-state river basins commissions, and various special commissions also engage in such efforts. To the Water Resources Council falls the major responsibility for coordinating their activities.

It should be acknowledged that President Carter and the Office of Management and Budget are currently seeking to increase their supervision over the planning of water projects.[34] However, the above agencies, rather than the President or Congress, dominate the planning. Such efforts require a variety of skills in hydrological engineering, planning techniques and methodologies, and other specialized areas. In addition to academia and private consulting firms, governmental agencies are the major source of this expertise. Few congressmen, presidents, and appointed officials are skilled enough.

Problems of Accountability

Given the predominant role played by governmental agencies in water resources planning, problems of accountability arise. The planners and other bureaucratic officials who perform such studies are not directly subject to popular control. Moreover, the task of ensuring the development of responsible water-related plans is increased by (1) the independent stature of several of the planning agencies, (2) certain characteristics of water resources planning, and (3) the particular political, organizational, professional, and personal factors that intervene in the planning process.

Stature of the planning agencies. Several of the agencies traditionally involved in water resource planning are powerful political actors. In addition to their expert knowledge, other factors are the nature of the services they provide, their strong interest-group support, and their own political skills. The Corps of Engineers, which enjoys broad Congressional support for its activities, is probably the foremost example. As Fried notes: "The Corps of Engineers builds flood control, water supply, waterways improvement, shore protection, and recreational projects throughout the country and can provide each and every Congressman with visible evidence of what that Congressman has done lately for his constituency."[35] The Corps is also supported by numerous interest groups, including the National Rivers and Harbors Congress—an unusually strong lobbying group comprised of key congressmen and representatives of industries affected by Corps' projects. Corps members themselves serve in an ex-officio capacity. Finally, as Elizabeth Drew notes, personnel of the Corps are astute politically, especially in their dealings with legislators.[36] As a result, the Corps of Engineers has gained Congressional approval for projects despite, in some instances, the opposition of the President, the Secretary of the Army, or the Office of Management and Budget (or its predecessor, the Bureau of the Budget).[37]

In practice, even Congress' scrutiny of the planning and other policy-making activities of agencies such as the Corps, the Bureau of Reclamation, and the Soil Conservation Service, is not rigorous. In its 1973 report the National Water Commission noted that if a representative or senator becomes interested in the authorization of a local project,

he can often command considerable resources in producing congressional action. Mutual respect for a colleague's constituency affairs and his acknowledged superior insight into what may be best for his district or State inhibit congressional resistance at this stage. With the aid of tacit rules of mutual noninterference and accommodation Congressmen have ordinarily been able to obtain authorization for local projects wherever there is substantial local support for them.[38]

Moreover, as one Bureau of Reclamation official has observed, the process of Congressional authorization

is our words coming back at us. In other words, we propose to do something at a certain place . . . We draft the authorization language in most cases. So authorization is a mere reflection of what we propose to do.[39]

It is possible that public support for such projects and the latter's political benefits may have diminished somewhat with the rise of environmental concerns, even that organized opposition to particular projects will arise, but at present these agencies are holding on to their political power and their independence.[40]

Characteristics of water resources planning. Certain aspects of the process also diminish the accountability of the bureaucratic officials involved in such efforts. First, because of the large number of interagency studies (and the plethora of agencies involved), responsibilities often overlap, making it difficult to trace the origins of various recommendations. Where state and local agencies are involved, the problem is compounded by the fact that the planning efforts typically cut across state and local boundaries.

Second, because of their highly technical nature, water-related studies are not readily subject to lay review. The reports themselves are frequently written in technical jargon difficult for political officials or lay citizens to read and comprehend. The length of many planning reports, which often represent several years of work, and the detailed level of analysis also impede legislative or citizen oversight.

Third, water resources planning involves dealing with potential benefits and costs which are difficult to quantify and imprecise at best, and individuals with different perspectives, assumptions, and methodologies frequently disagree on the calculations, even within the scope of a given study. This is particularly true when attempts are being made to quantify environmental and social benefits and costs. The building of the ill-fated Teton Dam, which collapsed in mid-1976, is a case in point. Knowledgeable individuals disagreed on a number of environmental and safety issues.[41]

For example, experts disagreed on the recreational value of the wilderness area which would be altered by the proposed dam.[42] The existence of such debates and the imprecision of the techniques used in water resources planning mean that there is no fixed body of knowledge by which agency performance can be judged. Even standards prescribed by federal laws and agency guidelines permit different interpretations.

Fourth, most current studies indicate that planning efforts that are linked to water-related concerns are of relatively low salience unless a particular crisis is involved. For example, Russell Dynes and Dennis Wenger, in their study of the perceptions of seventy-four community leaders, found among these individuals a distinct lack of awareness of and consensus regarding water-related problems.[43] The environmental movement has seemingly made many officials and the general public more conscious of water-related concerns than they were previously, but in the eastern United States the level of interest often remains low. Planning efforts are frequently future-oriented and less demanding of immediate attention than other public conerns. In such cases planners perform their tasks far removed from public attention.

Several aspects of water resources planning, then—the excessive number of agencies involved, the technical complexity of such studies, the methodological imprecision of water-related planning, and the often low salience of these undertakings—hamper the quest for accountability. These problems are not unique to water resources; nevertheless, one may identify other policy areas where fewer agencies, less technical language, more readily definable costs and benefits, or greater public awareness are involved. For example, policy-making in such substantive areas as housing, education, and defense are concentrated in fewer departments or agencies.[44]

Intervening factors. Political, organizational, professional, and personal factors intervene in water resources planning. First, political pressure is likely to be exerted upon bureaucratic policy-makers by key congressmen and by private concerns whose interests may be affected by planning recommendations. In practice, water bureaucrats are less accountable to the entire Congress than to the public works committees and appropriations subcommittees of both houses. For example, consider the successful efforts of the late Senator Robert Kerr (D-Oklahoma), a key member of the Senate Public Works Committee, in promoting a massive navigation project to provide Tulsa with an outlet to the sea.[45] Also, private local interests, especially barge companies, real estate agents, contractors, and industries, frequently join together—usually through a Chamber of Commerce—to request and support particular projects.[46] Thus political factors influence the water-related problems that will be studied and the recommendations of the planning effort once the study has begun.

Second, as discussed above, the organizational structure of the planning agency or its inaccessibility to the public may prevent a full discussion of the merits of a given study. Moreover, concerns for organizational betterment affect planning efforts. Rivalries between competing water resources agencies, such as the Corps of Engineers and the Bureau of Reclamation, are intense. The fact that planning may lead to subsequent involvement in more detailed studies or in construction (with more opportunities for the agency) also influences planning recommendations. Considering such pressures, the National Water Commission found it hardly surprising that "federal construction agencies tend to color their calculations with self-interest in making project evaluations."[47]

Third, professional factors intervene in water resources planning. A prominent role is played in such efforts by members of the engineering profession, a trend that has in part grown out of the long history of the Corps of Engineers in water resources development. In the eyes of many observers, the dominance of engineers has had a significant, but adverse, effect on water resources planning. Daniel Hoggan and his associates summarize this effect:

Engineers, reflecting their training and background, have basically approached planning problems as professional builders. Their training in engineering, mathematics, and the natural sciences has resulted in a tendency for them to adopt an axiomatic approach to problem solving that rarely led to questioning of fundamental postulates, particularly with respect to human behaviour. Consequently, water planning has characteristically emphasized structural solutions that were calculated to be the most efficient physically and economically. Mounting criticism of this type of planning in recent years has been that it does not include the consideration of non-economic values, such as aesthetic quality and social welfare. But a much more fundamental and crucial criticism is that few planners ever considered social solutions to planning problems.[48]

Similarly, Hoggan argues that water resources planners play a "confirming role." Using projections of past trends, they tend to focus on the future as a fixed state and plan to meet those needs.[49] Seldom do they consider the option of altering trends and thereby also the future needs for which they are planning.[50]

Fourth, administrative officials involved in water resources planning are subject to particularly strong personal pressures, which may influence their decisions. The salaries of many officials are charged directly to the planning studies and the construction projects in which their agencies engage, and their tenure in these agencies is dependent on the continuance of such activities. Individuals strive to create new roles for themselves and their agency.[51]

The force of these particular political, organizational, professional, and personal factors; the problems inherent in water resources planning itself; and the autonomy with which several planning agencies function—all underscore the need to increase the accountability of the bureaucratic officials who plan the use of the nation's water resources. At many junctures in the process, specialized concerns and interests confront administrators as they go about their policy-making activities. The presence of these lobbying interests reduces the likelihood that the water resources plans that administrators create will be lawful, responsive, and effective.

Although there is a need to hold bureaucratic officials answerable for the plans they formulate, in doing so care must be exercised. Measures designed to increase accountability may in the extreme stifle the creativity of individual administrators, deprive them of their individual dignity and opportunities for self-development, and thereby prove counterproductive.

Alternate Ways of Enhancing Bureaucratic Accountability

In seeking to increase bureaucratic accountability, in water resources or in other policy areas, authors have explored a variety of significantly different approaches. Various writers argue that the control of bureaucracy lies in the strengthening of the accountability of administrators to the Congress or the President, the courts or fellow bureaucrats, professionals or lay citizens. Each of the choices provides a potential way of increasing the accountability of the bureaucratic officials themselves.

Control by the Congress. Herman Finer, Joseph Harris, and many others look to the Congress as the institution best suited for holding administrators accountable.[52] They note that as a body of elected representatives, Congress is the appropriate institution for the task and possesses a variety of means for exerting control. It has power over substantive policies and programs and over agency budgets. In addition it can exercise control over the structure of public organizations, over personnel, and over the administrative procedures which agencies utilize. Oversight is practiced both by committees and by the General Accounting Office. Stemming from them are numerous informal means of control.

However, a variety of problems are associated with Congressional control of administration. Senators and representatives, even their staffs, may lack the information necessary to supervise bureaucratic officials, especially since the time of the former groups is divided among many activities. Control appears particularly weak when agencies and their supporters possess significant political resources and rewards.[53] Moreover, that Congressional power is fragmented—entrusted to committees and influential chairmen and other leaders—makes it likely that specialized interests can and will intervene. Given what has been said above about the relationship between Congress and the water resources agencies, these problems seem particularly severe in this policy area.

Control by the executive branch. Other observers, citing the President's powers as chief executive and commander-in-chief, his control over appointed officials, and the status of the Office of Management and Budget (OMB) as a policy coordinator and "clearinghouse" for legislation, have emphasized executive control as a means of increasing administrative accountability. The concern for centralization has long been a prominent theme in the literature of public administration. This was the thrust of the 1937 Brownlow Committee report and was repeated in the Hoover

Commission studies. In the area of water resources, the theme is reflected in the 1973 report by the National Water Commission.[54]

Yet critics have also challenged the feasibility of this approach. Richard Neustadt points out that Presidential power is not all-encompassing; it frequently depends on the Chief Executive's ability to persuade.[55] In practice, the record of the President, his appointed officials, the White House Staff, and OMB in controlling agencies is checkered. Executive control is limited by the size of the federal bureaucracy, by the system of separation of powers, and by the employment security which bureaucrats enjoy. In water resources the special relationship between the Congress and certain agencies, as well as the vast number of agencies involved in policy-making, hamper executive control.

Control by the courts. Reliance on the courts also offers an approach to enhancing bureaucratic accountability, for judges have a variety of means by which they can control agency activities. Walter Murphy maintains that the foremost of these legal instruments is "the authority to decide cases between parties, one or both of whom may be a state or federal official acting in the name of his government."[56] Judges also possess tools to carry out their decisions, including injunctions, declaratory judgments, writs of *habeas corpus*, and ability to cite individuals for contempt of court.[57]

In practice the use of the courts is slow and costly. Moreover, since court control of bureaucracy proceeds on a case-by-case basis, with particular emphasis on procedural requirements, there is often a lack of guidance on broad policy questions. For example, in cases dealing with the requirements of environmental impact reporting, the courts have focused more on the procedural requirements of the reporting process than on the substance of the reports themselves.[58]

Control by professionals. In a different approach, Carl Friedrich and other authors, including those in the school of the New Public Administration, have emphasized the accountability of bureaucratic officials to their fellow professionals. Friedrich has advanced the view that public officials must be responsive to two elements: technical knowledge and popular sentiment. Given the need for expertise, the task of determining whether a policy meets the first test, that it reflects the "existing sum of human knowledge concerning the technical issues involved," must fall to professional groups.[59]

This view is also central to the school of the New Public Administration. What distinguishes this latter perspective from the former, however, is its concern for social change and its resulting focus both on organizational change and on the personal commitment of professionals within public bureaucracies to achieve this end. Critical of the concern for efficiency that pervades bureaucratic theory, the authors of this school, such as George Fredrickson, seek to substitute for it the goal of justice, or "social equity."[60] To achieve that goal, the New Public Administration calls upon professionals in office to act as advocates for the disenfranchised members of society.[61]

Whether public administration can continue to function in such an atmosphere remains questionable. The pursuit of such vague goals is bound to engender debates and conflicts which professionals may not be able to resolve. Even more significant is whether, in the light of the criticisms of professionalism, these self-controls are adequate. The concern is appropriate in dealing with water resources professionals as well as with those in other policy areas.

Control by citizens. Finally, in order to increase the accountability of administrators, still other writers have advocated that citizens be more directly involved in public policy-making. As noted by Herbert Kaufman, this focus on public participation differs significantly from previous efforts to centralize control over administration in the hands of the President or to achieve a neutral and competent public service within the framework of the merit system.[62] It also encompasses a potentially broad range of activities, including both those in which citizens advise officials and those in which citizens actually make decisions.[63] This approach, too, is not without its critics, and the degree to which citizens can and should participate in administrative decision-making remains a source of confusion and controversy.

Given all these concerns with accountability, each of the alternate ways of enhancing responsible bureaucratic action deserves further study, as does the apparent tension between the differing approaches. The primary focus of my work is on public participation.[64] In the pages that follow, I assess the impact of citizen participation on three studies conducted by the New England River Basins Commission and on water resources planning in general. I seek insight into the role citizens can play in resolving the problem of increasing the accountability of bureaucratic policy-makers in such a way as to create more responsible water resource policies and other public policies.

CHAPTER TWO

The Rationale and the Experience

"Public participation" is both a theory whose merits scholars debate and a practice required by federal laws, executive orders, and agency guidelines.[1] For example, one can identify a substantial body of literature which explores the need for participation. In addition, given the present requirements for participation in water resources and other policy areas, the term possesses a growing empirical referent. In seeking to analyze the impact of public participation on the accountability of water resources planners, one must examine both of these dimensions—its rationale and the recent experiences in implementing the concept.

Although some attempts have been made by Daniel Moynihan and others to link more closely theory and practice, the efforts to implement public participation have outrun efforts to understand the varied implications of doing so or to evaluate the newly developed record of such involvement.[2] In particular, relatively few students of the problem have sought to analyze the rationale behind such activities.[3] Yet it is this rationale which guides attempts to implement the concept and provides standards by which such practices can be judged.

The Rationale for Public Participation

Generally speaking, the rationale for involving citizens in administration applies similarly to water resources and other substantive policy areas. What is striking, however, is the diversity of the arguments which proponents raise in supporting the concept.[4] Authors—whether academicians, administrators, or even agency clients—have approached the subject differently. The rationale for public participation consists of a number of arguments, not all of which are directly related or necessarily accepted by given proponents. Nevertheless, one can identify in the literature of public participation five prevalent reasons for integrating citizens into administrative decision-making. Public participation may be advanced as a way of (1) strengthening the bonds of community, (2) furthering individual self-development, (3) facilitating the implementation of public programs, (4) improving the quality of public policies, and (5) increasing government by the people, including the disadvantaged members of society.[5]

(1) *Participation and community.* From a sociological viewpoint, public participation affords one possible remedy for a serious problem confronting postwar American society, the erosion of the sense of community which human beings, as social animals, require.[6] Citing the works of William Kornhauser and Maurice Stein, Richard Cole argues that increased industrialization, bureaucratization, and urbanization, accompanied by changing familial and religious conditions, have loosened the bonds of American society.[7] The resulting danger is that other forces will move to fill this void and that citizens will, in Stein's words, "become increasingly dependent upon centralized authorities and agencies in all areas of life."[8] In the extreme, manipulation and totalitarianism could result. For these writers, then, citizen participation stands as a way of reversing such tendencies and restoring group identification.

(2) *Participation and self-development.* Authors like Pateman focus their attention on the individual citizen and his self-development, rather than on society as a whole.[9] In doing so they note that because existing inequalities in America's social structure impede genuine political participation, individuals have little control over their lives.[10] They lack, according to Bachrach, "the opportunity for development which accrues from participation in meaningful political decisions."[11] As a result, the human dignity and individual growth called for in classical political thought are absent under these conditions. Moreover, the realization that one cannot

influence government is likely to lead to a diminished sense of political efficacy and such related feelings as apathy and even alienation.[12] These authors argue, therefore, that direct participation by citizens in both the public and private (work place) sectors is necessary to alleviate the problems and permit individuals to realize their full potential.[13] Though restricted to the public realm (which is perhaps insufficient by Pateman's standards), the integrating of citizens into administrative activities addresses these needs.

(3) *Participation and policy implementation.* Still others, like James, focus on public participation as a means of facilitating the implementation of plans and policies.[14] Those adopting this approach are disturbed by the tendency of many plans, despite considerable expenditures of time and money, to gather dust on office shelves. As such delays are encountered, problems go unmet. This may be due to the complexity of the tasks, to the myriad of governmental units involved, or to opposition on the part of affected citizens.[15] Presumably, citizens will fail to support and will, perhaps, resist new policies unless they approve of (either really understand or at least trust in) the nature of the suggested change. Viewed from this perspective, public participation represents a way of overcoming the obstacles by preparing and mobilizing citizens so that they can take part in subsequent implementation battles, by fostering a trust between planners and citizens that will increase the latter's commitment for projects, and by helping to produce plans that are politically feasible and likely to be implemented.[16]

(4) *Participation and public policy.* Other proponents of public participation are primarily concerned with improving the quality of American public policies. As noted above, critics attribute many of the perceived deficiencies of current policies to their bureaucratic origins. In turn, such authors cite many potential gains to be realized from increased public participation. First, as noted by Harvey Frauenglass, the knowledge that citizens have about local conditions may usefully supplement the information otherwise available to planners and other administrators.[17] Second, citizen input may assist in identifying problems and solutions where such tasks are highly dependent upon social preferences and values.[18] Third, citizens with specialized backgrounds may provide expertise in certain substantive matters which exceeds that of the ad-

ministrators. Fourth, the demands voiced by participants may force administrators to take a more broad and more objective view of policy questions than is usually the case. Finally, closer public scrutiny may encourage more careful and thorough analysis. In these instances, greater public participation and better public policies go hand-in-hand.

(5) *Participation and democratic government.* Finally, public participation is seen by certain proponents as a method of enhancing democracy. As discussed above, administrative policy-makers are not readily subjected to popular control, yet are pressured to respond to a number of political, organizational, professional, and personal concerns. Public participation permits citizens to increase their voice in government. Unlike the traditional mechanisms of representative democracy, public participation allows citizens to be involved in decision-making, as advisers or actual decision-makers. For writers like Kotler, decision-making directly by citizens epitomizes democracy.[19] The integration of citizen advisers into administrative activities offers a more feasible if limited way of increasing citizen control over public officials. It also serves an educative function. Presumably, citizen participants will be better informed and able to carry out their other democratic responsibilities.[20] Although empirical evidence is weak in this regard, Almond and Verba's findings suggest that the participants' sense of political efficacy will rise following such involvement and that they will be encouraged to take part in other public activities.[21] In addition, public participation provides access for groups who have not otherwise been integrated into government. For example, advocates of public participation in the "War on Poverty" sought increased power for the black poor, so that the latter could obtain better services and a more equitable share of society's resources.[22] In these different respects, then, public participation fosters democratic government.

Despite differences of emphasis from one student to the next, these five views—that participation enhances community, individual development, implementation, the quality of policies, and democracy—comprise the logic for public participation. As such they form the underpinning of a concept that has currently gained wide application in water resources planning. Of these varied arguments, it is the last two which most directly address the need for bureaucratic accountability expressed above. To the extent that public participation enhances the quality of public policies and control by the citizenry, more responsible policy-making will result.

Assessing the Rationale

Because these arguments help to shape the role played by citizen participants and to determine the legitimacy of such activities, it is important to look more closely at their relative merits. Significantly, a survey of the related literature reveals challenges to virtually all the assertions found above. When such debates are taken into account, it is the arguments most directly related to bureaucratic accountability which emerge as the most compelling, though still contested, reasons for integrating citizens into water resources planning and other administrative activities. The remaining claims become less persuasive.

One can cite several reasons why public participation is unlikely to increase either community or individual self-development, the first being that participation has an apparently limited appeal to most Americans. Since few citizens participate in ways other than voting (and even then activity is confined to one or two issue areas), it seems presumptuous to say that citizen participation will become widespread enough to achieve these ends.[23] Secondly, it is unclear that participation responds to the essential causes of anomie or alienation. If one attributes anomie, as did Durkheim, to "the lack of rules to live by and the loss of values to pursue," this linkage seems improbable.[24] Even if one attributes anomie to the leadership of society losing its closeness to the people, citizen participation may not help to overcome such feelings.[25] Much will depend on the nature of the interactions that occur. Thirdly, as seen in the adoption of the Green Amendment (returning control over antipoverty funds to elected local officials), citizen participants find it difficult to wrest power from political elites. In short, the goals of community and individual self-development are too complex and elusive to serve as a basis for integrating citizens into administrative activities.

The argument that participation will facilitate the implementation of policy is also beset with problems. First, citizen participants may not be attuned to current political realities, in which case their contribution will not enhance the feasibility of the final plan or policy. Secondly, as the research of Daniel Mazmanian indicates, that citizens participate in planning does not mean that they will support a proposed project; their own values, which may remain unchanged by their involvement, determine whether support is forthcoming.[26] Indeed, where prior disagreements exist, participation may serve to crystallize opposition and thus impede implementation.[27] The most serious defect in this argument, however, is that it treats the act of implementation as an end in itself, diverting attention from the quality of the policy being implemented. In the extreme, efforts aimed at facilitating action and building public trust may be used to manipulate citizens into supporting proposed plans.[28] The potentially self-serving nature of this argument makes it the least satisfactory justification for public participation.

Despite the problems, public participation may be advanced as a means of enhancing both democratic controls and the quality of public policies; yet this argument, too, is not without detractors. More specifically, critics maintain that public participation will not advance the cause of democratic government because, as seen in the Community Action Programs of the 1960's, the small number of people involved will not properly represent the public at large.[29] Complicating the problem is the tension between citizen participation and other methods of providing accountability. To the extent that citizens legitimately influence decision-making, the responsibility of bureaucratic officials diminishes. The administrators become less answerable than before to the President, his appointed officials, the Congress, or the courts. If accountability to a relatively unrepresentative group of citizens is being substituted for these more traditional lines of control, democratic government is likely to suffer. In a different vein, authors who focus on democracy as an essentially electoral process argue that limited participation is healthy for the preservation of our political system, for it cushions "the shock of disagreement, adjustment, and change."[30] Robert Dahl argues, moreover, that lower socioeconomic groups, which now participate least in the system, have authoritarian tendencies that potentially jeopardize the democratic freedoms that Americans currently enjoy.[31]

Miller and Rein and other authors similarly question whether public participation will lead to improved public policy.[32] They perceive it to be a costly, time-consuming process that bears little fruit. Resources that could go into professional planning are diverted to participation activities, a pattern which Augustine Fredrich cautions could "result in public choices based on inadequate data and information."[33] Other concerns are that citizen participants, compared to administrators, lack the competence necessary to create effective policies and that they are more inclined to focus on parochial and immediate concerns.[34] Thus citizen participants may be a disruptive influence on both the policy-making process as a whole and the administrators personally.[35]

Although these critics raise important questions about the relationship between public participation and responsible public policy, certain of their criticisms are less cogent than others. For example, the argument that limited participation preserves stability ignores the needs of individuals who fare poorly under present distributions of power, and it therefore underestimates the desirability of change. Moreover, the argument seems short-sighted: the most stable political system in the long run is one that responds to the needs of its various constituent groups. More rather than less opportunity for participation seems likely to provide such stability. Similarly, even if authoritarian tendencies do exist among lower-class citizens, as Dahl contends, they seem to stem from feelings of exclusion from the political process. Increased participation might assist in changing such attitudes. That participation is not likely to be widespread does not negate its symbolic value in this regard, although, as noted, the ability of this sole mechanism to deal with such deep-seated feelings is suspect.

More serious are charges (1) that citizen participation is unrepresentative, (2) that it undermines other channels of accountability, (3) that it detracts from substantive policy-making activities, and (4) that it pressures administrators to respond to ill-considered recommendations. It is significant, however, that these arguments against public participation, like the arguments for it, are general and theoretical. Few authors have examined in any detailed way what public participation actually accomplishes in practice. Not surprisingly, then, little reconciliation of the competing arguments has occurred. At present, scholars disagree on whether public participation is likely to foster or impede efforts to create responsible plans and public policies. There is a need to examine the appropriateness of these competing claims in the light of recent experiences in implementing the concept. These experiences, in water resources planning and more specifically in the case studies below, should help us to gain insights into the relationship between public participation and responsible public policy.

Congressional Intent and Federal Requirements

Though citizen involvement in water resources planning is not an entirely new phenomenon, its nature has changed remarkably in recent years, because of new federal requirements for public participation. Demonstrations of local support have long been customary when an agency seeks authorization and funding for water-related projects, but citizen involvement in water resources *planning* was, until the 1970's, sporadic.[36] Interactions between citizens and planners varied considerably from project to project, often occurring late in the planning process. Not infrequently, the interaction has drawn criticism from observers, as in the case of the Tennessee Valley Authority when Philip Selznick charged that "grass roots democracy" really meant selling out to powerful local interests.[37] In contrast, public participation has become more deliberate and, in fact, a legal requirement. This movement gained impetus with the passage of the Economic Opportunity Act of 1964. As described by Daniel Moynihan, the inclusion of the words "maximum feasible participation" in that act set in motion a chain of events which led to public participation in the "War on Poverty."[38]

The participation phenomenon has since spread to other policy areas and levels of government. In water resources the trend was increased by the rise of the environmental movement in the late 1960's. Many environmentalists focused on citizen participation as a mechanism for injecting their concerns into the policy-making process. A document produced by the Bureau of Land Management summarizes the period as follows:

After years of seeming indifference, people were now taking responsibility for environmental preservation. They had become committed, and the news media's extensive coverage of their actions reinforced the whole phenomenon. In this context, it was politically opportune to write a national policy statement on the environment which recognized these concerns and a valid participatory role for the individual citizen.[39]

What is new about public participation in the 1970's is the unprecedented extent to which citizens have been integrated into the workings of public agencies. This is true in water resources planning, particularly at the national level, where numerous laws, executive orders, and administrative guidelines require public participation. Included are such major pieces of legislation as the National Environmental Policy Act (NEPA) of 1969 and the Federal Water Pollution Control Act (FWPCA) Amendments and the Coastal Zone Management (CZM) Act, both of 1972.[40]

Congressional perceptions of participation. Legislation suggests that the time was ripe for involving citizens in water resources planning, but one can identify other Congressional intentions behind the requirements. At times discussion of the merits of public participation proved less extensive than one might reasonably expect: neither the House and Senate reports on the CZM bill nor the law itself explained the rationale for the participation requirements therein, and attention elsewhere centered primarily on the rights of citizens to bring suit.[41] Nevertheless, the NEPA and FWPCA documents present various arguments for participation in administrative decision-making; it would help, for instance, to reflect public desires and generate valuable information. Sydney Howe, President of the Conservation Foundation, testified at the FWPCA hearings that greater participation was needed to end the "secret dialogue between the control agency and the polluter."[42] For the most part, however, citizen participation emerged as a means of ensuring that the environmental aspects of policies would be adequately assessed. For example, the Senate Interior and Insular Affairs Committee proposed in July 1969 that new means and procedures be devised "to preserve environmental values in the larger public interest."[43] Public participation readily gained acceptance as one such new means.

The case for public participation in environmentally related decision-making rested on at least three themes which recurred throughout the discussions over NEPA and the FWPCA Amendments. First was the concept that every individual citizen possessed the right to a clean and healthful environment. The involvement of citizens in federal actions affecting the environment became a logical extension of this right.[44] Secondly, proponents noted that because each individual has a significant impact on the environment, preservation "must depend upon the strong support and participation of the public."[45] Similarly, the Senate Public Works Committee, in favorably reporting the proposed FWPCA Amendments, stated that the implementation of pollution control measures depends "to a great extent upon the pressures and persistence which an interested public can exert upon the governmental process."[46] Thirdly, these various statements supported the argument that citizens possess information which can usefully contribute to environmental policy-making.

In general, then, Congress endorsed several of these theoretical arguments for participation. Citizen involvement was broadly perceived as integral to the formulation and implementation of responsible water policies. Proponents attributed a particular significance to public participation in this policy area. Primarily, it promised to provide for the adequate consideration of *environmental* concerns, thereby increasing the likelihood that resultant policies would be balanced assessments which reflected public needs and preferences.

The federal requirements for public participation. In any case, NEPA, the FWPCA Amendments, and the CZM Act clearly required public participation. For example, NEPA's statement of the rights of citizens to a healthful environment provided citizens with a broad legal basis for participation, and its requirements for the filing of Environmental Impact Statements gave them an avenue for involvement.[47] NEPA also called upon the Council on Environmental Quality to consult with the public in performing its tasks. In addition, Section 101(e) of the FWPCA Amendments provided for citizen involvement in the "development, revision, and enforcement of any regulation, standard, effluent limitation, plan, or program" established by the Environmental Protection Agency or the states under that act.[48]

Supplementing the provisions of these laws for citizen participation are two Presidential executive orders, E.O. 11472 and E.O. 11514, issued in 1969 and 1970, respectively. The former established the Citizen Advisory Committee on Environmental Quality; Section 2(b) of the latter called for the development of procedures "to ensure the fullest practicable provision of timely public information and understanding of Federal plans and programs with environmental impact in order to obtain the views of interested parties."[49]

These laws and executive orders, however, gave scant attention to the form public participation should take. To the agencies implementing the laws, especially the Water Resources Council (WRC), the Council on Environmental Quality (CEQ), and the Environmental Protection Agency (EPA), fell the task of developing procedures for involving the public. The more detailed requirements for citizen participation in water resources planning are found in the guidelines formulated by these organizations. The most far-reaching and definitive are the WRC's guidelines, found in its "Principles and Standards for Planning Water and Related Land Resources."[50]

Noting the importance of meeting needs and problems "as identified by the desires of people," the "Principles and Standards" directed planners to obtain public participation "through appropriate means of public hearings, public meetings, information programs, citizens committees, etc."[51] The WRC also observed that "direct input from the public involved at the local and regional levels" should be gained by:

a. Soliciting public opinion early in the planning process;

b. Encouraging periodic expression of the public's views orally, and recording their opinions, and considering them;

c. Holding public meetings early in the course of planning to advise the public of the nature and scope of the study, opening lines of communication, listening to the needs and views of the public and identifying interested individuals and agencies;

d. Making available all plans, reports, data analyses, interpretations, and other information for public inspection.[52]

In short, the "Principles and Standards" prescribed that a variety of mechanisms be used to involve the public in water resources planning and that they be employed early in and periodically throughout the planning process.

Although the term "citizen participation" potentially encompasses many levels of public involvement in decision-making, it is significant that the type of participation outlined in the "Principles and Standards" and these other sources is advisory only. The guidelines instruct water resources planners to consult with citizens and consider their comments, but the planners are not bound to accept the advice. And regardless of the precise role played by citizen participants, decision-making authority in water resources planning rests exclusively with the administrators and other public officials. This point is crucial in assessing the general impact of citizen participation and its specific effects on the accountability of water resources planners.

Achieving Public Participation

The general requirements and the rationale discussed above set the framework for public participation in water resources planning, but they afford little insight into how the concept has been implemented. Ironically, notes John Dixon, the vagueness of both the rationale and the requirements has led to a situation in which administrators themselves have been charged with designing a system by which others can hold them accountable.[53] It has been planners who, largely on a case-by-case basis, have integrated citizens into water resources planning through the creation of public participation programs tailored to their particular studies. To evaluate the role of citizen participants in such endeavors, one must examine the numerous efforts to implement the concept at the field level, and explore both the techniques currently used to provide public participation and the variables affecting their usage.

Fortunately, this task has been aided by the development of a specialized body of literature addressed to these concerns. Indeed, since the late 1960's scholars have studied attempts to make operational the concept of public participation in water resources planning.[54] At the heart of this literature are numerous case studies evaluating the use of one or more alternative participation techniques in particular planning efforts.[55] Others have sought to examine in detail specific techniques designed to facilitate participation or to develop an overview of the subject.

These studies reveal that the designs of public participation programs have varied considerably in terms of the specific techniques which planners have utilized. The broad range of the more widely used (traditional) techniques is exemplified in the following list.[56]

> Advisory committees or task forces
> Brochures, circulars, pamphlets, and workbooks
> Establishment of field offices
> Field trips and site visits
> Informal meetings with small groups and community
>   organizations
> Local planning units
> Mailings to potentially interested citizens and groups
> Mass media releases and materials
> Model demonstration projects
> Public displays
> Public meetings, hearings, and workshops
> Questionnaires or surveys
> Responses to public inquiries[57]

Typically, however, planners have relied upon the use of advisory committees, public meetings (of all kinds), the media, and communications materials which they themselves have developed. It is important, therefore, to examine the nature of these techniques, the manner in which they have been employed, and the advantages and disadvantages of each, as defined to date.

Advisory committees. The use of citizen, and at times science, advisory committees has been particularly widespread in water resources planning, although these groups have varied considerably in terms of size, frequency of meeting, and level of involvement. Though planners usually have striven to achieve a balance of different groups, selection procedures also have differed. Nevertheless, the merit of this technique lies in the opportunity it offers to a limited number of citizens to participate more directly in the planning process than they could through other avenues of participation. Experiences with these groups suggest, however, that performance depends greatly on the caliber of the citizens involved, their willingness to contribute substantial amounts of time to the activities, and the willingness of administrators to deal with them.[58] The history of this approach also suggests that particular problems accompany the use of these committees. In terms of the interests and demographic characteristics of its members, the groups tend to be unrepresentative.[59] The very closeness of the relationships involved may also lead to tensions between administrators and citizens if they disagree on issues or if the advisers feel that their recommendations are not being heeded. David Brown notes that the performance of advisory committees can be improved by clearly defining their mission, by developing staff assistance, and by improving their selection and operating procedures in order to provide a better mix of establishment members and other interest groups.[60]

Public meetings. Public meetings have also proven to be a flexible tool for integrating citizens into water resources planning efforts. Planners have at times utilized formal public hearings to solicit citizen comments. These normally provide a transcribed record, but allow for little citizen-planner dialogue. On other occasions, as in the "fishbowl planning" approach in the Corps of Engineers' Seattle District, planners have held informal public meetings or workshops in order to facilitate such interaction.[61]

In general, experiences indicate that public meetings perform two basic functions: they inform those who attend about the details of planning projects, and they provide individuals with an opportunity to voice their concerns. However, the technique gives rise to various problems. The citizens attending meetings often lack basic information about the planning investigations, especially if studies are at an early stage.[62] Like advisory group members, the citizens attending are frequently unrepresentative of the general public. Attendance fluctuates greatly. Finally, many citizens demonstrate at these meetings a local orientation at the expense of regional concerns. In light of the problems, Ann Widditsch emphasizes the importance of distributing information prior to the meetings and of advertising the meetings, to maximize turnout.[63]

Mass media techniques. Most planning studies also make use of the media in their public participation programs. Given the budget limitations of planning studies, the primary effort of most planning staffs has been to obtain free coverage by issuing "news releases" of noteworthy events. Some planners have exercised other options, such as appearing on scheduled radio and television programs. Probably the greatest coverage in terms of substantive information about the planning studies has been through the newspaper.

The use of the media is significant in that it permits the planners to inform large numbers of citizens about planning activities and to announce other participation opportunities, such as public meetings. Nevertheless, as Bishop points out, the use of the media does not of itself usually provide direct involvement, although some methods for establishing two-way communication do exist.[64] Also, to the extent that planners rely on the use of press releases, the final decision on what is printed is made by the media staffs, and coverage of crucial events may be inadequate. Suggestions for improving the use of the media in planning decision-making have been explored; Kahle and Lee, for example, stress the importance of taking local attitudes into account in designing programs.[65]

Staff communications materials. In addition to utilizing the media to reach the general public, many planning staffs have developed their own communications materials, such as notices of upcoming meetings, fact sheets, brochures, and summaries. Once they have established a mailing list, planners frequently send such materials directly to potentially interested individuals. They may also be distributed in bulk to individual groups or at public meetings. In practice, the quality of these materials and their distribution vary considerably.

With ample distribution, the use of such materials permits planners to reach a broad audience and in so doing to retain control over how the information is presented. The developing and mailing can be expensive, and frequently the methods have produced only one-way communication; however, as exemplified in the Corps' "fishbowl planning," this approach *can* be used successfully to foster two-way exchanges.[66] A number of studies have used their own questionnaire to seek public feedback. The various devices may invite citizens to make contact with the planning staff. James Hanchey observes that the methods seem potentially useful in determining public priorities and attitudes, a task recognized by all as being exceedingly difficult.[67] With that goal in mind, Wagner and Ortolano urge planners to expand their use of brochures designed to provide feedback.[68]

In general, the participation programs of water resources planning investigations have incorporated a mixture of these techniques at well-defined stages of the studies.[69] However, even where similar strategies have been employed, the level of participation has varied greatly from one study to the next. As Warner observes, different dimensions of these techniques may be emphasized, and planners have alternatively used them to inform and educate the public, to gain reaction to specific proposals, or to generate a broad interaction between citizens and administrators.[70] Planners have had different resources at their disposal. Still other factors which have caused variations in participation include the degree to which citizens (1) are aware of the issues involved, (2) perceive themselves as being affected by the decisions, (3) believe that they can influence decisions, and (4) feel that it is worth the effort to do so.[71] These variables in turn are likely to be affected by the geographical and functional scope of the planning investigation, the seriousness of related problems in recent years, the activity of interest groups in the area, and other, distinctly local or regional, conditions.[72] One finds a general consensus that public participation cannot be assumed but must be cultivated through well designed, somewhat aggressive programs begun early in the planning process.

This specialized literature usefully documents many recent efforts to integrate citizens into water resources planning. It also provides insight into both the advantages and disadvantages of the participatory techniques currently employed by planners and the variables affecting such activities. Moreover, it suggests but does not explore the likelihood that different mechanisms are appropriate to and needed for different cases. What most of these studies do not do, however, is broadly assess the actual impact of public participation on the varied planning investigations. The vast majority of the authors cited have apparently accepted participation as given—perhaps because of the numerous federal requirements now in place. Their evaluative comments have often been restricted to statements preferring certain techniques over others.[73] Even when writers offer suggestions for improving public participation, they typically fail to consider such reforms within the context of the basic rationale for citizen involvement. Their analyses are devoid of a theoretical base and do little to advance or reconcile the competing arguments. Because of this present state of the art, more analysis of the effects of public participation on water resources planning is needed.

In summary, the most compelling arguments for public participation are that it will enhance both administrative accountability and the quality of public policy. Given this logic and its refinement to include particular environmental concerns, public participation in water resources planning has become mandatory, widespread in practice, and, indeed, much studied. However, because of, on the one hand, the general nature of the theoretical treatments of this subject and, on the other hand, the narrow focus of studies that examine the application of the concept, two basic investigations are needed. First, we need to examine more systematically how the employment of participatory techniques affects the realization of positive goals envisaged for public participation. Does citizen involvement, in practice, enhance bureaucratic accountability and the quality of water resources plans? Secondly, if public participation is judged worthwhile, how can the techniques used to integrate citizens into administrative decision-making be improved in order to achieve the goals desired? These questions are examined in the chapters that follow.

Three Studies of Public Participation

Water resources planning is an extremely detailed and complex activity. In exploring its intricacies and the role that citizen participants can play in the process, the following analysis utilizes a case-study approach, focusing primarily upon the New England River Basins Commission (NERBC) and three largely autonomous planning programs run by that organization.

Nationally, the NERBC is one of six regional commissions created to coordinate public decision-making concerning the use of water and related land resources. As noted, a host of agencies at all levels of government have traditionally engaged in water resources planning. An apparent consequence of this multiplicity of effort has been that plans and policies have frequently been disjointed, at times even conflicting.[1] One approach to this problem has been the use of interagency coordinating committees, frequently under the leadership of the Corps of Engineers. This method of coordination is still prevalent in the South. The creation of river basins commissions represents a second, though not radically different, approach.[2] The New England River Basins Commission (NERBC), on which this study focuses, exists to coordinate the many state, interstate, and federal organizations involved in water resources planning in its host region.

The NERBC came into being with the signing by President Johnson of Executive Order 11371 on September 6, 1967. This action, in accordance with Title II of the federal Water Resources

Planning Act of 1965, followed requests for the creation of the Commission made by the New England Governors' Conference and the Governor of New York. (The geographical scope of the NERBC, which was modified soon after its inception, encompasses the New England states, the North Shore of Long Island, and the Housatonic River Basin in New York.)[3]

Organizationally, the Commission's membership includes representatives of ten federal agencies, six interstate and regional agencies, and the six New England states, as well as New York (identified in Table 1). Its operating budget, which was $380,000 for fiscal 1976, is borne by both the federal government and the member states.[4] NERBC also receives separate appropriations for carrying out special planning projects. The leadership of the Commission similarly reflects this federal-state partnership. The NERBC's Chairman is a Presidential appointee; the Vice Chairman is a state member. The Commission itself meets quarterly, often in two-day sessions, while the Chairman and a staff of about forty people carry out the day-to-day administrative responsibilities of the organization, primarily from NERBC's office in Boston, Massachusetts.

The duties of the NERBC and its staff are fourfold: (1) The Commission, as mentioned, serves as the principal agency for co-

TABLE 1. *Members of the New England River Basins Commission*

State	Federal	Interstate
Connecticut	Department of Agriculture	Atlantic State Marine Fisheries Commission
Maine	Department of the Army	
Massachusetts	Department of Commerce	Connecticut River Valley Flood Control Commission
New Hampshire	Department of Health, Education and Welfare	
New York		Interstate Sanitation Commission
Rhode Island	Department of Housing and Urban Development	
Vermont		Merrimac River Valley Flood Control Commission
	Department of the Interior	
	Department of Transportation	New England Interstate Water Pollution Control Commission
	Nuclear Regulatory Commission	
	Environmental Protection Agency	Thames River Valley Flood Control Commission
	Federal Energy Regulatory Commission	

SOURCE: New England River Basins Commission, *A State-Federal Partnership*, pamphlet distributed by NERBC, Boston, undated, p. 11.

ordinating water and related land resource plans on a regional basis. For example, staff members provide technical planning assistance to state personnel. (2) It prepares and updates regional plans for developing these resources. (3) It is charged with recommending long-range planning priorities for the region. (4) It recommends and undertakes planning studies on problems of regional importance.[5] In these various ways it seeks to improve the management of the region's resources so as to: "provide a healthy attractive environment fit for man to live in, while at the same time supporting an economy which provides decent opportunities for the people of the region."[6]

Conducting planning investigations has proved to be an important function performed by the NERBC, as it has in other regions also. Since its inception, NERBC has sponsored or cosponsored a variety of such studies, like one examining the economic and environmental effects of off-shore oil production and shipment.[7] More importantly for this analysis, NERBC has also played a leadership role in several major subregional comprehensive planning programs, three of which have recently been completed. These include studies of water and related land resource problems in the two-state Long Island Sound area and the three-state Southeastern New England area. A third and more restricted study focused on reduction of flood damage and flood-plain management in the four-state Connecticut River Basin. These investigations are referred to below as the Long Island Sound Study (LISS), the Southeastern New England (SENE) Study, and the Connecticut River Basin Program (CRBP) Supplemental Study. All three are classified by the Water Resources Council as Level B studies. As defined by the Council, a regional or river basin (Level B) plan is a

preliminary or reconnaissance-level water and related land plan for a selected area. These are prepared to resolve complex long-range problems identified by less detailed studies such as framework studies and the national assessment. They may vary widely in scope and detail, but will focus on middle term (15 to 25 years) needs and desires and involve Federal, State and local interests in plan development. They also identify and recommend action plans and programs to be pursued by individual Federal, State and local entities.[8]

Origins

The three studies all began during the early 1970's. In all three concerns expressed by citizens and public officials furnished the original impetus. In the Long Island Sound area, worries about water-related problems voiced by many individual citizens, officials, and organized groups in the late 1960's led Senator Abraham Ribicoff (D-Conn.) to hold three public meetings to evaluate the situation. These meetings demonstrated broad public support for a thorough examination of the Sound's problems.[9] Following the Ribicoff hearings, NERBC approved an initial program for studying the Sound, and in January 1971 the Water Resources Council authorized the Commission and its member agencies to prepare a detailed planning guide for the study of the Sound's water and related land resource problems. With the assistance of interim citizens and science advisory committees, NERBC developed, approved, and published this document.[10] It called for a three and a half year study, costing about three million dollars. Officially, the study began on July 1, 1971; because of delays in funding, however, it did not open its New Haven, Connecticut, office until April 1972 and did not get fully under way until later that year.

SENE began in a similar way, with similar funding delays. Following two years of discussion, Congress appropriated money for fiscal year 1970, but it was impounded by the Bureau of the Budget until January 1, 1971. Throughout this early period the New England Governors' Conference strongly supported the study. Once funds were received, the plan of study commenced and was published in April 1972.[11] As with LISS, an Interim Citizens Advisory Committee assisted the staff in formulating recommendations regarding a permanent advisory group structure for SENE.[12] To complete the inception of the study, a SENE office was opened in Boston, Massachusetts.

The background of the CRBP Supplemental Study is somewhat more complex. It followed and supplemented a 1970 comprehensive study of the Connecticut River Basin, conducted by a Coordinating Committee which was directed by the Corps of Engineers.[13] Considerable public criticism of the nine-volume Corps' report accompanied its release. Citizens objected to its recommendation for building seven dams in the Basin and to a perceived lack of consideration of environmental and social impacts which would result from these and other proposals. Such public comments drew support from Representative Silvio O. Conte (R-Mass.) and other legislators.

When, as prescribed, the Corps distributed the report to other public agencies for a 90-day review period, the newly established New England River Basins Commission appointed a Citizens Review Committee (CRC), composed of scientists, businessmen, and interest-group members, to assist it. The CRC proved itself to be a highly competent panel, and their report was generally applauded. Bernard B. Berger attributes this to the following conditions:

The charge was clear and specific; the issues were important and timely; the members of CRC were well-informed on these issues; a time limit of 90 days provided a useful spur to Committee effort; NERBC's Chairman gave unstinting encouragement and support; and the media's attention was focused on the Committee. In addition, the skepticism concerning the impartiality of CRC expressed by a very highly motivated group of "concerned citizens" (Connecticut River Ecology Action Corporation) provided a further incentive to produce a well-reasoned set of recommendations.[14]

Significantly, the CRC's report also criticized the inadequate examination of environmental impacts in the Corps' study and called for the further study of such concerns.[15]

The Commission reported its findings on the Comprehensive Study in *The NERBC 1980 Connecticut River Basin Plan.*[16] Generally, it acknowledged the above criticisms and recommended another study to reexamine the flood management plans developed by the Corps. The *1980 Plan* also called for the inclusion of both citizen and science advisory groups in the follow-up planning program. The CRBP Supplemental Study began officially on July 1, 1972. Responsibility for running it was assigned to the small staff of NERBC's Connecticut River Basin Program, which maintains a field office in Hanover, New Hampshire.

Organization of the Studies

Significantly, LISS, SENE, and CRBP involved a team approach to planning. Although the NERBC's own staff personnel guided and dominated the process, participants from the broad range of agencies comprising the Commission's membership played an important role. This can be seen in the funding. NERBC's share for each study was approximately 17 percent for LISS, 20 percent for SENE, and 28 percent for CRBP, all high figures by general level B standards.[17] Other money for the studies went directly to the associated agencies, such as the Soil Conservation Service and the Corps of Engineers. The NERBC staff had no control over these expenditures. This working arrangement, which reflected the nature of the NERBC, necessitated a rather complex organizational structure, an understanding of which is important to examining the role of citizen participation and the accountability of the administrators involved.

Atop the structure stood the NERBC, which set broad policies. It also reviewed and passed final judgment upon the preliminary reports for the studies. Once it had adopted these reports, the Commission sent them to the Water Resources Council for forwarding to the President, Congress, and the state governors and legislatures. It also requested necessary personnel and funding to perform the studies and, where necessary, reallocated those funds at its disposal.

Each study had its own Coordinating Group, which met quarterly over a one- or two-day period. These Groups, headed by the Chairman of NERBC, consisted of representatives holding policy-making positions in the agencies involved in the respective studies. The Coordinating Groups for LISS, SENE, and CRBP made basic policy decisions within the context of the studies and dealt with substantive questions which arose. The Coordinating Groups also reviewed reports prior to their submission to the Commission, made personnel and budget recommendations to the Commission, and coordinated the work of all agencies associated with their study.[18]

In each study, a Study Management Team, consisting of the study manager, his staff, and representatives from the agencies, met quarterly.[19] The Team focused its attention on coordinating operational matters. Members were generally more actively involved in the mechanics of the planning process than were the Coordinating Group members.

The day-to-day planning efforts of LISS, SENE, and CRBP were carried on by NERBC staff personnel assigned to each study and the planners in the various associated agencies who shared a similar role. NERBC's own personnel formed the core staffs for the three studies. These LISS, SENE, and CRBP staffs consisted of a study manager, one or two professional planners, a public information specialist, and varying numbers of assistants and secretaries. These staffs in effect managed the planning programs. They assumed responsibility for compiling the work of the associated agency planners, for writing the draft and final planning reports, for directing the citizen participation programs, and for conducting the routine business of the studies from their respective offices.

The planners from the associated agencies performed many of the substantive planning tasks needed for the studies, such as gathering data, identifying problems, and formulating and analyzing alternative action proposals. In doing so, the agencies performed specific tasks assigned to them in the plans of study. Agencies working in the functional areas of LISS and SENE—for example, recreation and transportation—met periodically in work groups to coordinate their efforts. Each work group, under the direction of a lead agency, produced a joint report for use by their study's staff in plan formulation.[20]

These work groups and the individual agencies coordinated their activity closely with the staffs of the studies. Numerous telephone conversations filled the voids between meetings. This was also true of the relationship between the LISS, SENE, and CRBP staffs and their respective Coordinating Group and Study Management Team members. Despite the lack of fiscal control over the associated agencies, the LISS, SENE, and CRBP staffs, by nature of their roles in the studies, could at times influence agency activities. The staffs also could directly supervise the performance of a limited number of planning tasks performed by private consulting firms or by NERBC's own central staff.[21]

Objectives of Citizen Participation

Public participation was in fact integrated into the complex planning processes of LISS, SENE, and CRBP. At their inception

NERBC explicitly recognized the need for citizen involvement. Several factors helped to account for this. The NERBC chairman himself, prior to his involvement with the Commission, had served in a leadership capacity with a well known conservationist group and was therefore accustomed to working with the public and was disposed to do so. It was also clear from the start that citizen participation would in the near future become mandatory in such planning efforts. In addition, staff personnel realized both the strong traditions of participation and the sophistication of interest groups in New England.[22] Finally, NERBC's successful experience with the Citizens Review Committee may have encouraged this outlook.

To assess citizen participation, let us begin by examining the expressed objectives of citizen involvement. These objectives are significant for three reasons. First, since they presumably guided the planners in the studies, they may provide insights into the logic followed by the public participation programs. Second, the objectives can be evaluated for their appropriateness and their completeness. Third, they can be used potentially as a framework for evaluating the programs as they evolved.

The objectives of citizen participation in the three studies can be found in the LISS and SENE *Plans of Study* and in the *1980 Plan*, as well as in various staff memoranda.[23] Although these discussions are by no means identical, they do provide a comparable overview of the subject. As one examines them, one finds a variety of objectives, some of them similar to those discussed earlier.

An objective of public participation by citizens and scientists was to provide information about local conditions in order to supplement the knowledge of the planners. As stated in the LISS *Plan of Study*, its purpose was "to make use of the knowledge of people who live near the Sound and who are close to its problems."[24] This same source acknowledged that users of the Sound "have a close working knowledge of the area that will be a valuable aid to the study team."[25] In a related vein the LISS *Plan of Study* also stated that scientists, by contributing their own information, might have a similar impact.[26]

The *1980 Plan* identified a second objective of citizen participation—the development of management plans "that are responsive to public needs and preferences."[27] Although neither the SENE or LISS documents were quite so explicit, they also viewed public participation as a way of identifying and exploring a broad range of viewpoints and values. At a minimum this theme suggested that citizens could make planners more aware of values. At a maximum, as in the *1980 Plan*, it recognized that public participation could potentially enhance the responsiveness of government.

Given the assumption that most citizens are not aware of water-related problems, the study documents viewed the educating of citizenry about public problems and proposed solutions as a third objective of citizen participation. This objective sought to enable citizens to participate more meaningfully in the planning process—perhaps to facilitate achieving the first two objectives, or perhaps to build support for implementation.[28]

The last-named also found expression in the study documents. The SENE *Plan of Study* saw citizen participation as a means "to provide citizen commitment to the final plan through active involvement in actual plan formulation processes."[29] A fourth objective was, then, to increase the likelihood that plans would be implemented. Some observers might view the pursuit of this objective by an agency as a form of cooptation. Clearly, however, NERBC's intentions were more honorable. Since the Commission's legal mandate limited its activities strictly to planning (as opposed to implementation), its efforts to generate action on the plans were not aimed at providing a continuing role for the organization in the implementation process.

Collectively, these NERBC documents stated that citizen participation should be pursued in order to (1) supply administrators with additional factual information about local conditions; (2) indicate to planners the values and preferences of citizens; (3) inform citizens about public problems and alternative solutions; and (4) facilitate the implementation of the final plans. These objectives required public participation programs designed to provide a two-way dialogue between planners and citizens. Ideally, the planners would provide sufficient information to the citizens, so that they could participate meaningfully in the studies; the citizens would provide the staffs with feedback in regard to their preferences and assessments and with additional information. Given

C.1

such an interaction, citizen participation would result in technically sound, responsive plans that would in all likelihood be implemented.

These objectives for citizen participation in LISS, SENE, and CRBP closely resemble those comprising the general rationale for participation, discussed above. The one exception is that the study documents do not mention the value of participation to individuals in terms of their own self-development. It is also true that these early texts did not systematically examine the implications of the objectives. For example, the documents did not elaborate upon the potential impact of the objectives on the democratic nature of government in New England or New York State; they focused more on the mechanics of how to involve the public in the planning process. Significantly, the role of citizens in supplementing the factual knowledge of the planners received a more forceful statement in these materials than in much of the literature of citizen participation. (This subject is pursued below, in Chapters 4–6.)

In general, however, the LISS and SENE plans of study and the *1980 Plan* presented only superficial examinations of the objectives for public participation; ostensibly, in themselves they provided little guidance to the planners and citizens involved. The discussions of participation in the NERBC documents do suggest, nevertheless, that the broad goals for participation listed above are readily applicable to these three studies.

The Public Participation Programs

In order to evaluate the public participation programs of the LISS, SENE, and CRBP staffs, one must understand the nature of the planning processes used in the three studies. Particularly important is the fact that the scope of the three studies dictated a long and complex planning process, one which agency guidelines divided into six discrete steps, namely (1) problem assessment, (2) establishment of objectives and plan evaluation criteria, (3) plan formulation, (4) plan evaluation, (5) plan reformulation and reevaluation, and (6) plan selection.[30] Highlighting these last stages were the publishing of LISS, SENE, and CRBP draft reports; their review by federal and state agencies, local and regional officials, and the general public over a 90-day period; and the issuing of final reports by the respective staffs (subject to approval by NERBC). However, decisions made throughout the earlier planning phases also shaped these resulting products, the final plans. For citizens to participate in such complicated planning investigations to the maximum extent feasible, their involvement in each of the steps would be necessary. This standard is used below in assessing public participation in the three studies.

To integrate citizens into their operations, the LISS, SENE, and CRBP staffs utilized public participation programs comprised of numerous related elements. These programs, which proved similar in all three studies, included the use of citizens and science advisory groups, three series of public meetings, and a variety of other communications strategies. Responsibility for carrying out the programs rested with the public participation coordinator and, ultimately, with the manager of each study. The three public participation coordinators served full time, although their talents and the demands upon the three staffs led to their involvement in substantive planning activities. The public information officer for the Commission assisted these individuals at various junctures. Given the importance of the participation programs in channeling citizen involvement in the studies, it is appropriate to examine their various elements in greater detail.

The citizens advisory committees. At the heart of the participation program of each study stood an active regional Citizens Advisory Committee (CAC). These committees numbered thirty and thirty-two members in the LISS and CRBP Studies. The SENE CAC, which operated more informally, had approximately thirty-three members.[31] During their most active period, the advisers to CRBP and LISS met monthly, and those associated with SENE met quarterly. At the suggestion of its interim advisory committee, SENE provided for a second level of involvement by the establishment of twelve Basin Advisory Committees.[32]

Despite the formal adoption of this two-tiered advisory group structure by the SENE Study, the differences here between that program and LISS and CRBP proved to be largely semantic. In practice SENE's Basin Advisory Committees consisted of individuals who attended open sessions comparable to the public meetings, or workshops, held in the other studies. These sessions were simply public meetings. One finds, in fact, that the CAC's of all three studies operated similarly.

NERBC chose the members of these committees by elaborate procedures. In LISS the governors of New York and Connecticut each appointed eight members, and the NERBC chairman selected fourteen. Similarly, in CRBP the four governors each appointed six members, and the chairman picked eight. SENE utilized a different formula. The chairman initially picked nine at-large members and later appointed two additional members selected at each of twelve public (Basin Advisory Committee) meetings held throughout the region.

In all three studies the staffs, with the help of interested groups, generated lists of suitable individuals. These lists guided NERBC and the various governors in making their selections, but their compiling and the formalities of appointment caused considerable delay in selecting advisory committee members. Observers of LISS reported that in New York gubernatorial appointees were screened at the local level, a time-consuming process.[33] New Hampshire also delayed its selection of CRBP citizen advisers. Finally, the filling of all positions on the SENE CAC had to await the holding of the first series of public meetings. As a result, in all three studies the CAC members entered the planning process somewhat later than intended and did not fully participate in the early phases of planning.

In selecting these CAC members, the staffs of the three studies and of the Commission sought to draw upon individuals of diverse interests and backgrounds. For example, the LISS *Plan of Study* called for an advisory committee representing:

conservation interests	youth and the elderly
commerce and industry	low income groups
outdoor recreation	historic and cultural interests
public health	transportation and utilities
planning and design professions	local government
academic interests	state legislators[34]

Ideally, NERBC envisaged a citizens advisory committee in each study which would reflect the broad range of interests of different segments of the public with a stake in water resources planning.

In practice such a broad mixing of interests did not occur. Low-income citizens and minority group members displayed virtually no interest in joining these bodies, although a black member (a professional) became the first chairman of the LISS CAC. Time and monetary considerations may also have limited participation in the CAC's by low-income as well as moderate-income people. Reimbursement for travel and related expenses offset some of the monetary costs of involvement. However, the fact that CAC activities required substantial investments of time and that meetings typically occurred during the day precluded many citizens from becoming involved, even if they had desired to do so.

Some people oriented toward business concerns did become members of the CAC's and active participants in the planning processes, especially in LISS. But the potential impacts of the planning programs on business affairs did not seem sufficiently important to stimulate the broad interest of business people in the CAC's or in the studies themselves.[35] On the other hand, individuals oriented to conservationist and environmental concerns showed considerable interest in LISS, SENE, and CRBP and equal willingness to participate in their CAC's. As noted, citizens sharing such concerns were in part responsible for the initiation of the CRBP Supplemental Study.

As for the advisers' personal characteristics, a 1974 study by Madge Ertel found that the LISS, SENE, and CRBP CAC members were "relatively affluent, well-educated, professionally and organizationally active, and well experienced in the kinds of issues related to the study programs."[36] Nearly 40 percent of the advisers surveyed had received graduate degrees. About 60 percent of the advisers had average family incomes exceeding $20,000 per year, with over 30 percent exceeding $35,000 per year.[37] The groups contained a disproportionate number of men, although the SENE committee—which had the fewest women members—did have a woman chairperson. Most of the women associated with the studies either were at that time or had been active in the League of Women Voters, which has a demonstrated interest in water resources.[38]

These findings indicate that CAC members represented neither a broad range of substantive interests nor a cross-section of the citizens living in the three regions. Most of the members displayed a distinctive, in some cases long-term, interest in environmental concerns and proved better educated and more wealthy than the average. In these senses they were, as the literature suggests, unrepresentative. Their profile also reveals that they brought to the studies considerable knowledge about the topics at hand.

The level of involvement of these advisers in the three studies varied significantly from one individual to the next as, over the course of the investigations, a self-selection process began to operate.[39] Many of the CAC members became unwilling or unable to continue a commitment to the studies over a three- to four-year period. As a result, active participation in the committees' activities diminished over time. The second chairman of the LISS CAC reported that a nucleus of about seventeen or eighteen members (out of thirty) actively participated in the committee.[40] Committee rules provided for the replacement of inactive individuals, but that was not done. Numerous resignations and subsequent reappointments occurred in all three studies but especially in CRBP, where the turnover rate exceeded 50 percent. An added factor in this case may have been the limited focus of that study. Because the reappointment process followed the same procedures as for the initial selection, the staffs encountered delays in filling vacancies on the committees.

Such events are not uncommon in long-standing volunteer groups.[41] New priorities intervene, and the interests of active individuals may shift. Also, several members initially may not have understood how long standing a commitment was being asked of them by the three staffs. One member reported that he had not been consulted prior to his appointment.[42] At least one resigned in protest over the course of the planning investigation, a rare occurrence. Clearly, however, this self-selection phenomenon had implications for the three participation programs. As noted by Madge Ertel: "it meant that those members who did choose to participate actively were in a position to exert a weight of influence which distorted the 'balance of interests' which was the objective of the appointment process." [43] It must also be kept in mind that certain individuals, though generally inactive, may have participated at critical points, and by other means than attending meetings.

Advisory committee members who did participate actively engaged in a broad range of activities. The plans of study and later memoranda assigned several types of functions to the CAC's, such as:

(1) helping to guide the planning process by identifying goals and objectives, major issues, and public preferences;
(2) reviewing the working documents and the final planning reports of the studies;
(3) facilitating general public awareness of and contribution to the studies, by communicating with other individuals and groups; and
(4) aiding in the adoption and implementation of the studies' plans. [44]

With varying degrees of emphasis and success, the LISS, SENE, and CRBP citizens advisory committees performed these duties. Their role in the implementation process, however, goes beyond the scope of this investigation.

CAC members did, indeed, provide on-going supervision of the planning programs. In LISS and SENE the advisers formulated lists of objectives to be pursued by the staffs. [45] Individual members attended not only the regular CAC meetings, but work group, Study Management Team, Coordinating Group, and Commission meetings as well. However, involvement in the activities of the work groups, though encouraged and coordinated by the staffs, proved to be uneven and somewhat sporadic. Only some individuals chose to participate to this degree, and frequently those who did complained that they did not receive sufficient information from the groups. [46] In general, CAC members reviewed considerable amounts of study materials, including working documents and draft reports, which were forwarded directly to them. They frequently responded to these individually by mail or phone, as well as collectively at meetings. In the SENE Study the CAC chairman regularly visited the staff's office and was integrated into staff operations. Many CAC members played an active role in all three studies. The results of their activities are described in Chapter 4.

CAC members in all three studies also undertook numerous activities intended to broaden public participation in the planning efforts and to foster communication with other interested parties. As the Ertel survey revealed, CAC members perceived this communications function as an important activity.[47] Apparently staff members did too. All three CAC's organized public information subcommittees to facilitate public involvement in the studies, and these groups, as well as individual members, expended considerable energy developing linkage between the staffs and the public at large.

In an indirect sense CAC members fostered public involvement in the studies by adding the names of local residents to the studies' mailing lists, reviewing general informational materials, helping the staffs to interpret comments made at public meetings, and arranging meetings between the staffs and local leaders. They aided the staffs in identifying citizens to invite to the first public meetings. They also assisted the planners in ascertaining whether public materials and presentations at meetings were sufficiently clear and free of technical jargon, so that citizens could readily comprehend them. This latter activity took place in both committee and subcommittee meetings and occurred prior to the first and second series of public meetings more than before the third rounds of meetings. One related problem which arose on several occasions was that the staffs did not distribute the materials early enough to give adequate time for CAC review.[48] It should also be noted that the LISS CAC frequently pressed the staff for more publicity about the study, but without any demonstrable effect.[49]

More directly, CAC members spoke to individuals and groups about the planning projects, sent articles and letters to local newspapers to publicize the studies, and helped to organize and run many of the public meetings. The first two types of activities reflected individual initiative, since the staffs made no systematic attempt to use CAC members as spokesmen. It is likely that they considered such a strategy risky, given their lack of control over individual CAC members. Nevertheless, CAC members assisted in selecting the cities and towns and particular facilities where the meetings were held, and in some cases they made the meeting arrangements. Excluding the final series of public meetings on LISS and SENE, the staffs integrated the CAC members into such activities as moderators or discussants. Many CAC members did not attend these functions, however. CAC involvement in the final series of meetings of LISS and SENE proved limited, and the people attending spoke as individuals rather than as representatives of the CAC's.

It is difficult to evaluate the success of CAC members in finding citizens who would participate in the studies. Responses to the questionnaires used in my research indicate that 21.3 percent of the citizens attending the final series of public meetings in the three studies had personally discussed the studies with a CAC member and that this figure was considerably higher for CRBP (28.2 percent) than for LISS (17.0 percent). After controlling the CAC members who themselves attended the meetings, these figures decrease by several percentage points. Using this indication, one finds that fewer than 20 percent of citizens attending the meetings who were not themselves CAC members had discussed the studies with members of the CAC's. The responses also indicate that government officials attending the meetings were more likely to have been in contact with CAC members than were other citizens.[50] This suggests, in turn, that CAC members played a somewhat limited role in directly informing other citizens about the studies, although this activity proved more successful in CRBP and in reaching local governmental officials.

The CAC members, then, helped to inform other citizens about the studies by (1) facilitating citizen-planner contact; (2) reviewing public materials; (3) helping to arrange, and participating in, public meetings; (4) generating publicity; and (5) informally discussing aspects of the studies with other individuals. Their direct communications with others were circumscribed, but this does not detract from the value of their indirect informational activities. The impacts of the latter are impossible to assess precisely, but more systematic use of CAC members in this regard was possible.

In general, rather small, selected groups of citizen advisers actively participated. Although they represented a narrow cross-section of interest, they were well informed on water resources issues. Given this knowledge, they played a major role in guiding the planning process and informing other citizens about the studies.

The science advisory committees. In each of the three studies a science advisory committee also participated in the planning process. These science committees were labeled "the Research/Planning Advisory Committee" (R/PAC), the "Regional/Scientific Task Force" (R/STF), and the "Science Advisory Group" (SAG) in LISS, SENE, and CRBP respectively. They numbered twenty-nine members in LISS, eight in SENE, and thirty-seven in CRBP. Unlike the CAC's, these science committees did not all operate the same way. LISS's R/PAC, which perceived its role to be quite different from that of the CAC, functioned independently of that body.[51] It met as frequently as once a month, at times using a seminar format. In SENE the opposite occurred: the small R/STF and the regional CAC formed a collective entity which met on a quarterly basis. The CRBP citizens and science advisory groups met separately for a time and later jointly, at monthly intervals. In all three studies the science advisers made substantial contributions as individuals apart from the group meetings.[52]

The members of the science advisory committees were appointed because of their professional backgrounds. Most but not all taught at colleges and universities in New England and New York; they had a broad range of specialties applicable to the studies. In contrast to the selection of the citizen advisers, the NERBC chairman appointed all the science advisers. As a result, in both LISS and CRBP, the science committees began operating before the CAC's did. With R/PAC, R/STF, and SAG, as with the three CAC's, a self-selection process began immediately, and as a result the working membership of the committees was much smaller than the original totals.

Here, too, other commitments may have intervened, or the scientists may have become disillusioned because of the complexity of the studies or their uncertain roles. This self-selection process occurred most rapidly in CRBP, where the precise nature of the study took considerable time to evolve. In commenting upon CRBP's Science Advisory Group (SAG), Bernard Berger observed:

such groups are not very effective unless the charge given is clear and specific, and of a nature amenable to approach. Put in another way, I believe SAG could have been more effective if well-defined problems were presented to them. This is not the way it worked. The members of SAG were asked to carry on a continuing review of an evolving plan to anticipate problems. This process produces a welter of possibilities whose evaluation and screening are time-consuming and uncertain. Almost inevitably special studies are recommended. Such studies normally would require funding support. I believe many SAG members dropped out because they felt they could not make an input beyond identifying areas requiring special study.[53]

It is difficult to say what impact the self-selection process had on the behavior of the groups. In CRBP it appears to have been the "hard" scientists, the specialists, who dropped out, leaving behind generalists who shared broad, ecological concerns.[54] On Long Island, the research-oriented scientists lost interest as the study progressed. Nevertheless, a number of scientists remained active throughout their tenure on the committees.

They, like the CAC members, engaged in a broad range of planning activities, which had been defined earlier in the plans of study and other initial documents and included:

(1) using their knowledge to assist in the studies, especially by coordinating them with related research;
(2) identifying tasks requiring special studies, possibly by outside consultants, and facilitating this research;
(3) outlining long-term research agenda for the study areas; and
(4) discussing and, if possible, reconciling issues concerning the methodologies and results of the studies.[55]

With considerable variation from study to study, all three science advisory committees pursued these tasks. Their efforts are described and evaluated in detail in the next chapter.

The science advisers, then, brought to three studies considerable expertise in a variety of professional fields. A simplified selection process led to their early involvement in the studies, although many individuals were unwilling or unable to sustain this commitment. Those who remained active did perform a variety of tasks, some of which were similar to those of the citizen advisers and some required more technical expertise.

The public meetings. The LISS, SENE, and CRBP staffs used numerous public meetings to involve citizens. The format and timing of these meetings were similar in all three programs. For example, each of the studies held three series of public meetings at comparable stages in the planning process. A first series of meetings, held early when problems were being assessed and objectives defined, served to make citizens aware of the studies and to gauge their general preferences and priorities with respect to water-related issues. A second round of meetings was held at the midway point of the studies, when alternative solutions were being formulated. These sessions permitted citizens to examine and respond to initial alternative recommendations being developed by the planners. Finally, a third round of meetings during the official 90-day review period for each study gave people an opportunity to evaluate the draft planning reports.

In total, the LISS staff organized and conducted thirty-one formal public meetings over the course of the three-year study—ten in the first series of meetings, thirteen in the second, and eight in the third. SENE and CRBP held thirty-three and twenty-seven meetings, respectively, which similarly were divided into three groups. Within a given series, the meetings were held in locations throughout the planning area within a relatively short period. Table 2 illustrates this format.

Attendance at these meetings varied considerably from study to study and from meeting to meeting. It proved greatest in the more densely populated Long Island Sound area, where about 900, 1800, and 580 individuals attended the meetings. Fewer people attended the CRBP and SENE meetings, with totals of about 1400 and 1200 respectively.[56] Of the three study areas, the Connecticut River Basin was certainly the least densely settled. That citizens in the SENE planning area lacked a regional identity made it difficult for the staff to stimulate public interest and participation in the program. This identity problem stemmed in part from the planning area being neither a hydrological unit nor a region in any

TABLE 2. *CRBP's Public Meeting Locations*

First Series October/November 1973	Second Series June/September 1974	Third Series February/March 1976
Middletown, Ct.	E. Hartford, Ct.	E. Hartford, Ct.
Windsor, Ct.	Northampton, Ma.	Northampton, Ma.
W. Springfield, Ma.	W. Springfield, Ma.	W. Springfield, Ma.
Brattleboro, Vt.	Keene, N.H.	Keene, N.H.
Hartford, Vt.	Brattleboro, Vt.	Brattleboro, Vt.
Littleton, N.H.	Hartford, Vt.	Lebanon, N.H.
S. Deerfield, Ma.	Littleton, N.H.	Whitefield, N.H.
	Claremont, N.H.	Claremont, N.H.
	St. Johnsbury, Vt.	St. Johnsbury, Vt.
	Groveton, N.H.	
	Greenfield, Ma.	

SOURCE: NERBC, *The River's Reach: A Unified Program for Flood Plain Management in the Connecticut River Basin*, December, 1976, p. 246.

other exclusive sense.[57] As exemplified in the final series of public meetings in Rhode Island, where fewer than one hundred people attended four sessions, Boston-based SENE had difficulty attracting followers in Rhode Island.

A number of individual meetings held by the three studies drew audiences of a hundred or more residents, but most proved less successful. The low points of participation occurred at meetings in New York City and Keene, New Hampshire; in the latter place only about a dozen residents attended. The LISS staff held the former meeting outside the actual boundaries of the study in an unsuccessful effort to reach national and regional interest groups based in New York. The latter meeting was held by the CRBP staff on the night of one of New England's worst snowstorms—in the winter of 1975–76. All three studies held most of their meetings at night in order to bolster attendance.

To attract people to the meetings LISS, SENE, and CRBP employed a variety of techniques. They circulated news releases to local newspapers and other media outlets in the study areas. These both informed citizens about the studies and announced the meetings. The coverage varied considerably. For example, the newspaper coverage prior to the final series of meetings in each study appeared most widespread for LISS.[58] Within each study variations also occurred. SENE obtained greater coverage in Massachusetts than in Rhode Island; within Massachusetts, publicity was greater in the Cape Cod and North Shore areas than elsewhere. Certain newspapers printed only portions of the releases, while others provided additional information. The schedules of the public meetings generally appeared only once, if at all, in a given newspaper.[59] Unlike the others, CRBP effectively used radio and television to announce its final sessions by scheduling a number of appearances by the study manager, agency personnel, and advisory group members on various news and talk shows.

Secondly, the staffs mailed materials directly to area residents to announce upcoming public meetings. In doing so they used internally prepared mailing lists, which included the names of citizens thought to be interested. Local, regional, and state officials and environmental groups were well represented.[60] The staffs added the names of individuals who had attended previous meetings. For example, prior to their final meetings LISS and SENE sent summaries of the draft reports, printed in the form of tabloid newspapers, to interested citizens.[61] LISS mailed over 500 summaries to public officials, interested citizens, and groups. SENE reported mailing 4,000 summaries, some of which were sent in bulk form to interested groups and organizations for distribution to their members. CRBP, lacking time and money, sent out approximately 1500 copies of the draft report itself, along with explanatory materials and a schedule of its final public sessions.[62]

The staffs supplemented these techniques with numerous informal contacts. In addition, SENE directly called better than 200 local governments in its planning area to inform them about the meetings nearest them. A survey of individuals attending the final meetings indicates that, of the three studies, SENE had the highest percentage of governmental officials in its audiences—slightly over 50 percent, compared to 39.2 percent for CRBP and 23.7 percent for LISS. Even more clearly, however, the survey results, as shown in Figure 1, attested to the importance of the direct mailing procedure. Of those attending the final meetings, 43.6 percent said that they had heard about the study by mail compared to 38.4 percent by newspaper, 38.0 percent by talking with other citizens, and 10.1 percent by radio or television. In SENE and CRBP

FIGURE 1. *How Citizens Heard About A Meeting*

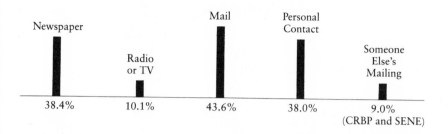

Newspaper	Radio or TV	Mail	Personal Contact	Someone Else's Mailing
38.4%	10.1%	43.6%	38.0%	9.0% (CRBP and SENE)

NOTE: Respondents could select more than one answer. Percentages add up to more than 100 because some citizens heard about the meeting from more than one source.

9.0 percent said that they had seen materials mailed to another individual.

These aggregate figures also demonstrate the importance of the newspaper in informing citizens about the meetings. In SENE, however, where only 26.2 percent of the respondents had heard about the meeting through this means, use of the newspaper proved of marginal utility. This was apparently due to the factors discussed above. The figure for the use of radio and television in motivating attendance was significantly higher (20.3 percent) in CRBP, reflecting that staff's more aggressive approach to these tools.

The survey also assisted in identifying the salient demographic characteristics of those citizens who had heard about the final series of LISS, SENE, and CRBP meetings and had chosen to attend. These citizens were both well educated and relatively affluent, as can be seen in Tables 3 and 4. Among the respondents, 37.7 percent indicated that they had done graduate work or received a graduate degree, while 13.1 percent reported an educational level of high school completion or less. Over a third of those participating in the survey (35.4 percent) stated that their annual family incomes exceeded $20,000. This figure proved highest in the LISS Study (40.5 percent). It is interesting that 9 percent of the respondents refused to answer the income question posed in the questionnaire. Overall the results are similar to those of surveys administered earlier by LISS and SENE. A LISS survey taken at the

TABLE 3. *Educational Levels of the Respondents*

		High School or Less	Some College or College Degree	Graduate Work
LISS	N	51	221	172
	%	11.4	49.4	38.5
SENE	N	37	165	148
	%	10.4	46.5	41.7
CRBP	N	58	152	102
	%	18.4	48.1	32.3
Total*	N	146	538	422
	%	13.1	48.1	37.7

* 1.0% missing observations.

TABLE 4. *Annual Family Income Levels of the Respondents*

		$8500	$8500–$13,000	$13,000–$20,000	$20,000
LISS	N	37	67	129	181
	%	8.3	15.0	28.9	40.5
SENE	N	32	57	118	124
	%	9.0	16.1	33.2	34.9
CRBP	N	29	55	97	91
	%	9.2	17.4	30.7	28.8
Total*	N	98	179	344	396
	%	8.8	16.0	30.8	35.4

* 9.0% missing observations.

meetings in the spring of 1973 revealed that about 35 percent of those attending had professional or graduate degrees, and nearly 50 percent had family incomes of over $20,000 per year.[63]

Although the survey of the third round of meetings did not examine the racial characteristics of the citizens participating, attendance by minority group members was virtually nonexistent, and the staffs acknowledged this situation.[64] No representatives of identifiable minority groups spoke at any of the meetings.[65] These conclusions are reinforced by the first LISS survey, during which 609 (95.9 percent) respondents identified themselves as Caucasian, 9 (1.4 percent) as black, 1 (0.1 percent) as Puerto Rican, and 16 (2.5 percent) as other.[66]

The general survey also indicated that citizen participants were actively involved in public affairs. A total of 39.1 percent had attended one to five other public meetings or hearings in the past year, and 44.8 percent had attended more than five. These figures are higher for governmental officials than for nonofficials, reflecting that public officials typically attend many meetings, but they remain high for both groups. As noted, the public meetings were attended by a disproportionate number of public officials, especially those at the local level. Over a third (36.7 percent) who answered the questionnaire held an elected or appointed office in government, primarily in a city or town. In SENE this was true for 50.7 percent.

The task of examining the attitudes and interests of the respondents was interesting but was limited by the small size of the questionnaire. The respondents, for example, exhibited a strong preference for local involvement in water resources planning. The majority of the respondents in each study felt that planning decisions concerning the use of water and related-land resources should be made primarily at either the local or regional level or by local and state governments working together. Very few favored state or federal primacy in such a role. Indeed, a concern for home rule surfaced at many meetings.

For the SENE and CRBP meetings an additional item on the questionnaire examined the one major concern (among five alternatives posed) in which each respondent was most interested. As noted in Table 5, the results indicated that those participating in the survey were primarily interested in concerns about the environment and community betterment. Several individuals commented that they viewed these two categories as related. Relatively few respondents were primarily interested in industrial or com-

TABLE 5. *Major Concerns of Respondents*
(by percent)

	Environ-ment	Industry/ Commerce	Private Property	Community Betterment	Recreation
SENE	42.8	1.7	3.4	19.4	2.3
CRBP	36.4	4.4	20.6	21.8	0.6

mercial problems in the narrow sense, apart from community betterment. In responding to a related question used in all the questionnaires, fewer then 10 percent (9.7) indicated any industrial or
commercially motivated interest, regardless of priority, in the
studies' recommendations. Respondents at the CRBP meetings reported particular concern for private property. This apparently reflected the study's recommendations, which potentially affected
property rights and values in flood-prone areas.

Finally, the survey provided an opportunity to assess the participants' knowledge about the studies. At the SENE and CRBP meetings, about half (52.7 percent and 44.6 percent respectively) reported that they did not know enough about them to be able to
offer comments at that meeting. This seemingly reflected the fact
that fewer than one third (31.0 percent) had attended an earlier
public meeting sponsored by the studies. These figures are also a
reminder of the expertise which administrators alone possess.

In general, then, individuals who attended the LISS, SENE, and
CRBP meetings displayed a variety of characteristics which set
them apart from other citizens. They were particularly well educated, affluent, active, and involved in local government. Few were
minority group members. They were oriented toward concerns for
the environment and their community rather than business per se.
About half considered themselves inadequately informed about
the studies.

The extent to which those who attended meetings actually participated in the planning process varied from individual to individual. Some sat and listened and, perhaps, responded in some way
after the meetings; others made statements or asked questions
ranging from very superficial to quite specific or detailed.

The activities undertaken at the meetings varied also with the
ways in which the meetings were organized. The LISS and SENE
staffs in their earlier meetings adopted a workshop format designed to engage citizens in small group discussions which addressed given concerns and which utilized special materials prepared with CAC assistance. Both LISS and SENE administered
questionnaires to supplement oral comments by participants. In
the LISS Study the staff had distributed one questionnaire at its
first meetings in the spring of 1973 and had included a second in

an issue of the *Urban Sea*, a staff publication, printed in the spring of 1974. This latter survey was designed to be completed at the second series of meetings or mailed to the LISS office. These questionnaires provided the staffs with information about the demographic characteristics and preferences of participating citizens. However, design problems, as pointed out by CAC members and other observers, limited the utility of the first LISS questionnaire.[67]

The final series of public meetings in the LISS, SENE, and CRBP Studies followed a similar format but differed somewhat in their tenor. Each meeting began with a presentation, complete with slides, which summarized the draft report. Following this, the study manager called upon citizens to present their comments. In LISS the staff conducted this final meeting in the manner of a formal hearing. Little interaction occurred between the staff and the citizens, because the staff rarely responded to the public comments. At the SENE and CRBP meetings, which were generally smaller, considerably more two-way communication took place. Also the SENE and CRBP meetings differed from those of LISS in that the staffs focused their presentations and slides more on the problems in the local areas where the meetings were being held. Despite such variations, all the meetings held throughout the three studies encompassed two distinct activities: the staffs provided basic information about the studies to the participating citizens, and the citizens presented their comments about the studies to the staffs. The nature of these comments and their impact on LISS, SENE, and CRBP are examined in the next chapter.

In summary, citizens other than the members of the citizens and science committees also participated in the planning processes of each study at three rather distinct intervals by attending public meetings conducted by the LISS, SENE, and CRBP staffs, at times with the assistance of CAC members or other public agencies. The staffs utilized a variety of means to attract citizens to these meetings, but not all segments of the public responded. Low-income people and minority group members did not genuinely participate in the meetings. Nevertheless, a substantial record of public comments was built up.

Other participation techniques. The LISS, SENE, and CRBP staffs also used other communications strategies, primarily to inform the public about their studies. The magnitude of these undertakings did not, however, approach that of the above efforts, nor were the techniques comparably used in all three studies.

Among the three programs, only LISS produced its own newspaper publication (*Urban Sea*), which appeared four times during the study. Its second issue contained, as noted, a public questionnaire, and its fourth and final issue consisted of a summary of draft plans for the Sound. Fifteen thousand copies of the last summary issue were circulated in the region, many at the final meetings. As reported by Jenene Geerdes, the *Urban Sea* issues contained both attractive and unattractive design features and were costly, but provided a great deal of information about LISS and a continuity with its public participation program.[68] Although neither SENE nor CRBP used this informational device in a comparable way, all three studies on occasion distributed brochures and other public materials.

LISS also organized a speakers' bureau, to provide staff presentations for interested community groups. The CAC played a minimal role in this activity. In practice the staffs of LISS, SENE, and CRBP all gave presentations of study-related topics to interested community organizations, such as Chambers of Commerce. All three staffs also arranged additional meetings with key interest-groups (though not with minority groups) to discuss the studies. In addition, CRBP, prior to certain of its public meetings, arranged discussion sessions with local officials and community leaders.

Finally it should be noted that the staffs frequently communicated with individual citizens in the planning areas in a variety of informal ways—in person, by phone, and by mail—particularly during the 90-day review periods. Thus individuals participated in the studies outside of the structured activities discussed.

LISS, SENE, and CRBP, for a broad range of reasons, sought to involve citizens in the three studies. Because the planning processes were so long and complex, they evolved elaborate, traditional mechanisms, including advisory groups, public meetings, and other communication techniques. Participation through public meetings was restricted to a few well defined stages. For the most part, those participating were people of means and education who were primarily concerned about a relatively narrow range of interests, largely environmental. In terms of their demographic characteristics and substantive interests, they were not broadly representative of the public at large. Lower-income, minority, and, to a lesser extent, blue-collar individuals were not effectively involved. Nevertheless, a recent study by Lester Milbrath demonstrates that lower-income people and blacks do have distinctive preferences and feelings about water resources questions.[69] It should be noted that other participation techniques, such as random sample surveys, which may have helped to discern the attitudes and interests of such groups, were not employed by the staffs.

Although these problems existed, many citizens availed themselves of the opportunities to participate, involving themselves to varying degrees and with varying amounts of information about the tasks at hand. It remains to examine the actual impact of those who did participate on the three NERBC studies, and the effects of their involvement on the accountability of the administrators associated with these planning programs.

CHAPTER FOUR

Participation and the New England River Basins Commission Plans

In order to assess the effects of citizen participation on bureaucratic accountability in the Long Island Sound, Southeastern New England, and Connecticut River Basin Program studies, we must examine the actual impact of citizen contributions to the three planning processes and their final plans.[1] Perhaps the most critical tests of citizen participation are in what it achieves in terms of public policies, policy outputs, and actual program accomplishments. Yet this is a linkage that has seldom been explored, with regard to these particular studies or any other similar planning efforts.

Such an exploration is a difficult undertaking. The scope of the interactions between the citizens and the planners was enormous. Also, the citizens had an impact on the studies through a variety of both formal and informal mechanisms, such as advisory group meetings, public meetings, meetings with private organizations or interest groups (or their leaders), and letters, phone calls, or visits to the study offices. Not all of these interactions, including private conversations between interest-group leaders and staff members, could be observed. Thirdly, citizen recommendations in some instances paralleled those of agencies or individuals who were members of the study itself; subsequent impacts cannot be solely attributed to the public. Fourthly, at times different groups, such as the citizens and science advisory committees, took the same position on a particular matter. In these instances it is difficult to know how much influence to attribute to one group versus the other. Fifthly, given human nature, different people offered different explanations for particular events.

Within these limits, the following examines the impact of citizens on the planning processes and the plans of the three studies. The focus is primarily, but not exclusively, on the citizens' comments during the advisory group and public meetings conducted by the staffs and the staffs' responses to these inputs. Inputs have been documented in various minutes and reports. My discussions with various citizens and attendance at many of the activities supplement the formal records. The staffs' responses are gauged by changes in the planning processes and substantive changes in the planning documents. Interviews with staff members also helped to clarify these impacts. Since these studies functioned as distinct entities, they are treated separately below, beginning with LISS.

The Impact of Citizen Participants on LISS

Public participants had an identifiable impact on the planning process and the planning reports of the Long Island Sound Study. One can trace both certain staff activities and substantive portions of the planning reports back to citizen inputs. The task here is to identify this impact and its consequences for the Long Island Sound Study. However, because the CAC members, members of the Research/Planning Advisory Committee (R/PAC), and the other public participants differed according to the nature and the level of their involvement in the planning process, their impacts on LISS varied. These groups are therefore best analyzed individually.

Impact of the Citizens Advisory Committee members. Members of the CAC brought to LISS concerns for the nondegradation of the Sound, for swift action in confronting water-related problems, and for the evolution of governmental structures to manage the Sound's resources. In arguing for these and many more specific worries, the CAC influenced the planning process. While discussions of the CAC's role in LISS preoccupied advisory committee members during their first meetings in the fall of 1972, by its sixth meeting that December the CAC had begun to examine the substantive elements of the process.

In the months that followed, members focused primarily on several major issues raised in the Long Island Sound area, the goals of the study, and the initial reports produced by the work groups. A major debate in the region at this time centered on a proposed bridge over the Sound and an Environmental Impact Statement on that structure released by the Metropolitan Transportation Authority. Although the LISS staff did not initially address the bridge issue, the CAC adopted a negative stance on the project and called upon the NERBC to oppose it.[2] After much delay and considerable persuading by the CAC, the Commission did so. This, then, was a successful effort by the CAC both at focusing the staff's attention on immediate concerns, even during an early stage of plan formulation, and at broadening the scope of the study beyond its original purview.

Early in 1973 the CAC produced a very general statement outlining goals for LISS, thus beginning one of the major tasks assigned to it in the *Plan of Study*. Later in November, at a two-day meeting, the citizen advisers drafted a more detailed statement of the problems existing in the Sound region and the CAC's goals and priorities for the study. The LISS staff studied this document, called "Goals for the Region," and distributed it to all other members of the planning team, urging their consideration of it.[3] As a result, this statement did have an impact on the study, although its effects varied considerably from one work group to another. Certain work-group leaders reported that they had incorporated the CAC-defined goals in their reports. Others found certain goals either too vague or, more frequently, too detailed to be used. The LISS staff and work group personnel also considered some goals to be outside the scope of the study; few were rejected solely on the basis that they were without merit.[4]

In certain cases this exercise had a direct impact on the study, in that it identified goals that had hitherto received scant attention. For example, the document on goals assigned a high priority to increased access for citizens, especially urban residents, to the recreational resources of the Sound—a concern ignored by the recreational work group up to that time. Subsequently the planners focused more attention on this issue. The LISS staff, which shared this broad concern, pressed the agencies in the recreational work group to address the problem of access, pointing out that the citizens perceived it as important. The CAC goals statement thus became a vehicle that assisted LISS planners in guiding the work groups in the direction that they, as well as the citizens, desired. In this instance the LISS staff used the goals document to enhance its weak control over the agencies in the work groups.[5]

During this period the CAC also began to review the inventory data and, later, interim reports of the work groups. Work-group leaders, the representatives of federal agencies, attended several CAC meetings and briefed the committee on their progress. With the assistance of the LISS staff, individual members also received reports of the work groups and attended work-group meetings. Although several CAC members complained frequently that work-group materials were not adequately circulated and that the citizens were not fully integrated into work-group activities, individual CAC members did have some impact on work-group operations.

One important example involved the participation of a CAC member, the owner and operator of a marina on the Sound, in the recreational work group. Based on his experience, this individual criticized the methodology employed to calculate the number of boats using the Sound. Over a period of several months the CAC, the LISS staff, the Corps of Engineers, and this individual discussed the issue; in the end the procedure was modified.[6]

The CAC members who became involved with the transportation work group met with less success in persuading that body to explore land transportation issues in its deliberations. The citizens argued that such concerns had a tremendous impact on the Sound, but the LISS staff and the other members of the planning team concluded that such questions lay outside the scope of their study.[7] Land transportation in the region was not studied in detail, although the final report and the Land Use and Marine Transportation reports briefly discussed these concerns—more than would have been the case without citizen involvement.[8]

Initially, the level of interaction between the planners and the citizens disappointed the CAC members. Frustrated by the perceived slow pace of the planning process and their difficulties in dealing with the work groups, the CAC formulated and then tabled a resolution to resign en masse.[9] The CAC withdrew this resolution at the next meeting because it felt that the study was progressing more satisfactorily and because, as one member reported, the CAC then recognized that to resign would end its opportunities to affect the study.[10] The CAC did, however, ask various legislators to examine their complaints. One staff member, who had worked extensively with citizen groups before, commented that he had never witnessed such an adverse relationship between planners and citizens.

These pressures were borne primarily by the LISS staff, but the other agencies felt them as well. In general, this episode provided an impetus for accelerating the pace of the study and for enhancing staff control over the associated agencies in the work groups. From this point on, relations between the CAC and LISS improved significantly.

During the next year and a half, the CAC focused primarily on specific proposals developed by the planners. At a meeting in early 1974 the members objected to several proposed sites for marina development. The staff eventually dropped two of these sites from the plan.[11] As the study progressed, the CAC also began reacting to the draft materials produced by LISS. In June of 1974 the CAC reviewed the preliminary draft of the "Plan Summary," especially the recommendation for centralizing petroleum receiving, storage, and distribution in the Sound region. The CAC supported this concept, although several members specifically objected to the proposed building of off-shore berths for tankers.[12] One later wrote a detailed letter to the staff arguing against such berths at one particular site. Although these comments did not result in basic changes in the recommendations, the staff in the final report discussed the pros and cons of the off-shore proposals. At the June meeting the CAC also criticized two recreational proposals which called for state acquisition of properties. The staff dropped these recommendations.[13]

Soon afterward the CAC reviewed the legal and institutional report produced by outside consultants. Members who had repeatedly emphasized the importance of interim and long-term management structures for the Sound endorsed the report, with some additional comments. They suggested that the staff clarify the importance of these recommendations for local governments and that the name "Long Island Sound" should be included in the titles of the new structures.[14] The staff followed this advice: the language of the management section of the final plan reflects the strongly felt concerns voiced by the citizen advisers.[15]

Following the release of LISS's draft planning report in late 1974, the CAC concentrated on reviewing this document. The outcome of this review was a CAC position paper which endorsed the study's draft recommendations across a broad range of substantive topics, such as flood damage reduction, mining, and commercial fishing.[16] CAC members again placed particular emphasis on the management recommendations. In other areas they approved of the general recommendations, with some significant reservations and exceptions.

The major criticisms offered by the CAC were that the staff should:

(1) grant more attention to the nutrient problem in the western Sound and to the goal of shellfishable waters;
(2) emphasize recycling wastewater on Long Island;
(3) focus more on the conservation of lands and less on their development for recreation;
(4) reconsider its recommendations for recreational ferries;
(5) set limits on the size of petroleum-carrying vessels entering the Sound;
(6) deal more fully with the subject of land transportation;
(7) drop its recommendations for reliance on nuclear power; and
(8) establish clearer priorities.[17]

The comments had an impact on the final LISS plan, although this cannot be attributed to the CAC alone. In many instances the citizens attending the last series of public meetings voiced concerns similar to those of the CAC, as did several R/PAC members. Citizen influence must therefore be attributed to all three groups.

Impact of the Research/Planning Advisory Committee members. Individually and collectively, members of R/PAC also had an impact on the Long Island Sound Study. Their contributions, which were not limited to their particular areas of expertise, reflected the dual role of the R/PAC members as both citizens and scientists. In many instances the R/PAC focused on broad policy questions regarding the Sound. As described by Madge Ertel, the members also sought to coordinate the study elements into a "conceptually meaningful, interdisciplinary whole."[18]

R/PAC involvement in LISS was highlighted by a series of "scientific seminars" held in the fall and winter of 1973. At these seminars R/PAC members presented formal papers on a broad variety of subjects related to the Sound, including land use, wetlands, mining, fishery management, power, the ecology of the region, food production, and transportation. These meetings, attended primarily by the scientists comprising R/PAC and a few staff personnel, served to promote both the discussion of the Sound's problems among professionals and the exchange of related information between various disciplines. In this sense the potential value of the seminars went beyond their contribution to LISS itself.

The influence of these R/PAC seminars and later meetings on the study varied among subject areas. Most observers and the staff acknowledged the particular influence of R/PAC's comments on the fisheries management section of the draft and final reports.[19] One R/PAC paper entitled "Prospects for Managing the Fisheries of Long Island Sound" was particularly important in this regard.[20] R/PAC recommendations called for a fisheries management program focused on resident species within the Sound, and clarified the need for more data. R/PAC scientists also criticized much of the available information on fisheries in the Sound as inadequate, and cautioned against approaching this section of the report in a manner that would promote sport fishing. The final LISS plan gave high priority to the establishment of a fisheries management program.

During these seminars R/PAC members identified other problem areas which they felt the staff should consider: access to the Sound, eutrophication in the Sound, the impact of New York City sewage on water quality, and land transportation. In particular they urged that the methodological limits of not including New York City in the boundaries of the study should be detailed.[21] Their call for "access," voiced also by the CAC, became a major concern. As one staff member indicated, however, the staff found R/PAC's emphasis on greater access in urban areas somewhat restrictive and preferred to think in terms of access along the entire coastline. The staff and the work groups responded to the other concerns by discussing these matters in their report. Several of the seminar papers were cited in the functional area reports. However, problems of timing adversely affected the use of the papers, for they dealt with broad concerns and prior to their completion the staff had begun to focus on more specific concerns.

During several meetings in 1974 R/PAC members commented on the initial draft recommendations being produced by LISS. Again they voiced concern about New York City's part in polluting the Sound, water quality in the western Sound, and land transportation.[22] In addition, they criticized the lack of priorities in the study—a broadly based citizen complaint. This last criticism did result in substantial reediting of the report by the staff. R/PAC's participation in the study waned during these later stages, however, in part because certain professionals lacked interest in the reviewing process. R/PAC made no effort to provide a collective written response to the final draft plan.

Impact of public meeting attendees and other participants. Other citizens also had an impact on LISS, by attending public meetings or by contacting the staff directly. The public meetings were held in three series between 1973 and 1975. As noted, citizens attending the first two series were asked by the staff to respond to two different questionnaires designed to measure citizen preferences.

The first series of meetings focused on five areas of major issues: electrical power, oil, water quality, recreation, and land use. Within these areas the staff sought to identify broad public attitudes, so as to guide later recommendations. In general the citizens' comments and their questionnaire responses demonstrated their support for more strict water-quality standards (even with a tax rise), for restricting growth, for opening new recreational sites, for reducing the impact of power generating and petroleum handling facilities on the Sound, and for preserving natural shoreline landscapes.[23] Environmental concerns received special support. The attendees did not agree on the desirability of state involvement in land-use decisions or of excluding nonresidents from local beaches.[24] For the most part, the staff acted in accordance with these broad preferences; however, because they were general and at times even contradictory, the direct influence of these early meetings on the study appears marginal. Part of the problem lay with the design of the questionnaire, which asked sweeping, unstructured questions.

During the second series of public meetings, citizens reacted to broad approaches to problems as well as to tentative, more specific proposals. Their comments generally reinforced the preferences expressed at the first meetings. Participants also supported the establishment of a coastal management program, cluster development, a fisheries resources program, and the centralization of petroleum-handling facilities.[25] They reacted negatively to certain other proposals, like those for a salt-water fishing license, certain recreational sites, and increased roads leading to beach areas.[26] The staff, as a result, abandoned the controversial fishing license proposal. It responded to certain of the citizen comments regarding recreational sites and activities, but not to others. In the final plan the staff emphasized the areas of agreement outlined above. In addition, comments made at one meeting and repeated later caused the staff to examine and adopt an option they had not previously considered: public acquisition of privately owned islands near one urban center.[27]

Public reaction at the third round of meetings, which followed the public release of the draft plan, proved to be more specific. Attendees' comments focused primarily on over a dozen broad recommendations and on the specific recreational proposals for given localities.[28] At several meetings the people present also criticized the alleged lack of publicity surrounding the study. Citizen comments supported LISS's draft recommendations in a broad range of functional areas[29] (see Table 6). These recommendations remained essentially the same in the final report. Other elements of the report drew a more mixed reaction. For example, while some residents approved of the study's call for increased state involvement in land-use management, others disapproved, objecting to any diminishing of local authority. These latter comments did not

TABLE 6. *Citizen Reaction to the LISS Draft Report at the Last Series of Public Meetings*

Elements of the LISS Plan Receiving Public Support	Elements of the LISS Plan Receiving Mixed Reactions	Elements of the LISS Plan Criticized
Water quality	Management proposals	No limit on vessel size
Port consolidation and pipeline extension	Public access	Artificial island
Flood control	Recreational ferries	Nuclear power
Water treatment and holding tanks		Lack of strategies and priorities
General approach and intentions	Recreational proposals— especially developed aspects	Acceptance of population growth

result in fundamental changes in the staff's management recommendations, although it did redraft certain portions of the report, pointing out the important role of and the benefits for local government in their proposals.[30]

Some citizens, in contrast to others who favored increased public access to the Sound, stressed concerns for private property. The staff's commitment to increasing access, which the CAC supported, did not diminish. LISS did reconsider its recommendations for particular recreational sites, although its response varied. In some instances the staff provided more details about its recommendations. In other cases the staff toned down its proposals, qualified them in other ways, or dropped them entirely—largely because of citizen as well as CAC comments.[31] Certain recommendations remained unchanged despite citizen comments. Also, as a result of public comments, the staff qualified its proposals for recreational ferries, emphasizing the need for more study.[32]

Citizens united in their criticism of several of LISS's draft recommendations and of the staff's perceived failure to consider certain problems or alternatives. Attendees at the public meetings, like CAC members, called for a ban on supertankers in the Sound. One former Coast Guard officer submitted an extensive brief arguing for a size limit on vessels entering the Sound.[33] The staff acknowledged this oversight and incorporated such a limit in the final plan.[34] The citizens attending the meetings also opposed, as did the CAC members, the study's endorsement of nuclear power. The staff responded by emphasizing energy conservation and by expanding the discussion of the pros and cons of nuclear power in the text of the final report; the call for new nuclear facilities remained, however.[35] Meeting attendees also criticized the plan's lack of attention to the subject of limiting growth in the region and lack of a strategy for action. These comments led to more discussion of population growth in the final report, although the staff felt it inappropriate to recommend limiting growth. The staff also revised the "Plan Summary," inserting more dates and cost figures, to add a better sense of strategy.[36]

In a variety of ways, then, the comments made by citizens at the public meetings had an impact on the final LISS report. The same is true with regard to the comments of the citizen and science advisers. Where the comments made at the public meetings and the CAC and R/PAC sessions coincided, they became mutually supporting. Overall, the staff incorporated numerous citizen comments in the LISS plan.

Impact of Citizen Participants on the SENE Study

As one examines the history of the Southeastern New England Study, it is possible to identify the particular impact made by advisory committee members and other public participants on the planning process, and the planning documents that resulted. Citizen participants in the SENE Study, as in LISS, had a distinct influence on the substantive content of the planning reports. However, as noted, SENE's CAC and its relatively small Regional/Scientific Task Force merged their operations. Since, in practice, they constituted one advisory committee, their impacts on the study are assessed jointly, below.[37]

Impact of the advisory committees. In general, the members of the Citizens Advisory Committee and the Regional/Scientific Task Force brought to the SENE Study a variety of general concerns. These included concerns for guiding growth in the region, for public access to recreational opportunities, for the conservation and nondegradation of existing resources, for using ground water supplies, and for local involvement in resource management. Interactions between the groups and the SENE staff reflected these concerns as did the final SENE report. However, the influence of the advisory committee members needs to be discussed in more specific terms in order to understand their impact on the study.

Although advisory committee members initially focused their attention on their own role in the study and their committees' internal operation, they quickly became involved in the more substantive aspects of the planning process. This started with their review of the socioeconomic and environmental base reports being prepared for SENE by the Economic Research Service and two other organizations. These reports sought to provide information about present and future conditions, so that needs could be addressed by the staff. The advisory groups took issue with the methodology used in the reports to make projections about population growth and with the accuracy of the figures developed. They also criticized the acceptance of identifiable trends as given quantities upon which planning should focus.[38] As a result, the SENE planners modified both the projections and the way in which they were used. From that point on, the staff emphasized a flexible approach to future needs.[39] The review also underscored the appropriateness of the staff's considering ways in which such trends might be altered.

The advisory committees kept abreast of developments within the region. For example, the committees passed a resolution calling upon the New England River Basins Commission to encourage Rhode Island's consideration of the proposed Big-Wood Reservoir in a statewide and interdisciplinary context. The Commission did so.[40] Even more important for the study itself during this period was the advisory committees' lengthy examination of SENE's goals and objectives.

At a two-day meeting at Woods Hole, Massachusetts, in late 1973 and in meetings throughout the spring of 1974, members of the Citizens Advisory Committee and the Regional/Scientific Task Force debated the appropriate goals and objectives for the study. During the initial meeting the SENE staff and Study Management Team members asked the advisers to identify and rank suitable objectives; they also revealed their own thoughts along these lines. A perceived lack of information and the ambiguity of the objectives suggested troubled the citizens, who pressed for explanations from the staff. Yet while advisory committee members expressed considerable dissatisfaction with the structure of the meeting, it did achieve positive results. It led to the identification of new concerns, such as with the location of power plants, and to the staff's reassessment and reorganization of its own previously developed statements.[41]

Following this meeting, a subcommittee from the advisory groups encapsulated these goals and objectives in a written report, the final version of which was circulated and approved in May 1974.[42] Nevertheless, the value of this process went beyond the importance of the six-page report itself. Probably the most significant benefit was in crystallizing staff perceptions of goals and objectives. In the next several months, SENE produced a draft planning report for the entire region and more localized reports for the ten planning areas into which the region was divided. Specific ideas generated by the advisory groups, with members acting jointly or individually, were incorporated in the documents. One member's comments, for example, led directly to the study's call for state-wide boating advisory committees to examine boating and marina needs. From this point until the end of the study, the advisory groups' activities centered on the review of these and subsequent draft planning documents. Three meetings—a two-day session at Plymouth, Massachusetts, in early September 1974, and two in 1975—were devoted to these concerns.

The Plymouth meeting afforded the advisory group members an opportunity to review the draft plan in detail. Four groups working simultaneously within different subject areas provided a point-by-point analysis of the draft report. Such comments made a particular impact on the land use sections of the plan, where the advisers criticized SENE's concept of confining development to five designated areas. The arguments of CAC and R/STF members that planned development should be spread more equitably to other areas prevailed. The staff later abandoned the concept of "development districts" in favor of the more general approach of "guiding growth."[43]

The citizen and science advisers also offered a broad range of other specific criticisms. A sampling of these include the recommendations that the SENE staff should:

(1) place more emphasis on the interrelationship between water supply and water quality;
(2) elaborate upon public rights to beach access;
(3) de-emphasize the concern for aquaculture;
(4) no longer recommend regional conservation commissions;
(5) not discuss time-zoning of beaches for fishing and swimming;
(6) call for swimming in reservoirs;
(7) identify more fully relevant decision-makers who will implement the SENE plan;
(8) reconsider the use of the word "preservation" where the intent is regulation; and
(9) modify its water quality recommendations to permit discharges that do not deteriorate the water quality of the stream.[44]

These and other proposed changes varied from fundamental to minor (editorial) recommendations. Most of the proposals were adopted outright by the staff and appeared in later reports. In a few cases they were not accepted, but even then, as with the "swimming in reservoirs" recommendation, the comments encouraged the staff to explore the issue and present the pros and cons in the text of their final report.

Similarly, the advisory groups made substantive recommendations at the following two meetings and by direct contact with the staff, and these comments were reflected in the planning reports. For example, at their advice, the term "unwelcome" facilities (for example, a refinery) became "key" facilities, a less pejorative term.[45] Further suggestions led to the staff's modifications of their outdoor recreational proposals. In their final meeting the committees also discussed the recommendations for the proposed Northfield and Millers Rivers diversions with a representative from the Connecticut River Basin Program's advisory groups. This, too, prompted the staff to qualify their proposals and to emphasize the need for the conservation of water.[46] In general, a broad range of proposals incorporated in the SENE Study reflect the impact, in full or in part, of the advisory group members.

Influence of public meeting attendees and other participants. Other citizens participated in the SENE Study by attending public workshops and meetings or by such other means as writing or phoning the staff. These citizens, too, had identifiable influence on the SENE plan. Indeed, their influence on the plan became more specific and easier to identify as the study progressed. This examination focuses primarily on the impacts of the workshops and meetings rather than on the less formal contacts.

It is difficult to discuss in concrete terms the effect of citizen comments at the first series of workshops, which began in late 1973. These meetings focused on the broad subject areas to be addressed by SENE, and the staff used a questionnaire to identify problems that concerned the public. The workshops demonstrated broad public interest in concerns associated with growth and the public's desire for action. In general, however, these meetings served primarily to inform citizens about the study and to involve them in it.

The comments made and questionnaires completed by citizens at the series of workshops in the spring of 1974 had a clearer effect on the planning reports. For example, citizens in the Ipswich–North Shore planning area of Massachusetts indicated their support for water conservation and for one large regional reservoir, rather than for three small reservoirs or the expansion of the Metropolitan District Commission water supply system. They also emphasized the need for greater protection of land in the upper portions of the Ipswich River. Subsequently, the staff incorporated these preferences in both the regional report and that particular planning area report.[47] In Rhode Island public comments addressed to the fragile nature of Napatry Point led to the altering of proposed recommendations for that area. In general, the workshop attendees demonstrated support for increasing wetlands protection and expanding beach recreational facilities. Strong opposition was voiced against providing public recreational access across privately owned land. These citizens, like the CAC members, also opposed the creation of regional conservation commissions.[48] The SENE draft reports later reflected these public inputs.

The most specific comments came at the eleven public meetings held in May and June of 1975 during the 90-day review period. There citizens reacted to specific recommendations in the draft reports, which had been released prior to this period. Their effect in this case can be assessed in part by comparing the draft and the final reports issued by the SENE Study.[49] In doing so, the impact of the citizens on a board range of topics becomes apparent. Recreational, water supply, and water quality issues were among the most frequently discussed concerns.

Considerable attention was paid to the study's recreational proposals, especially those calling for the development of present ocean-front parks, the acquisition of new beach areas, and the expansion of boating facilities. In general, the participating citizens shared the planners' concern for the problem of insufficient beach access for recreation. Specific projects proposed for the North-Shore area and the Boston Harbor Islands also received support. Local residents objected, however, to the study's recommendation for state acquisition of Duxbury Beach in the South Shore area and Quonochontaug Beach in the Pawcatuk area. They stated a clear preference for local or private management of these sites and questioned whether state agencies would protect the critical environmental areas along such beaches. As a result, the final report endorsed local control in the areas, provided that these resources were responsibly managed. Otherwise, the study noted, the subject of state acquisition would be raised again.[50]

Citizens at several meetings disagreed with the staff's call for increased boating facilities in the areas, as well as accompanying recommendations for channel dredging. Subsequently, SENE gave marina development a more cautious go-ahead. The planners adopted a new slant on this subject by focusing on the possible expansion of existing facilities rather than the construction of new marinas, as the way of accommodating boating demands.[51] The staff foresaw such studies being done in conjunction with the boating advisory committees suggested initially by a SENE advisory committee member.

Likewise, the public supported SENE's water quality recommendations. One individual cautioned the staff on its proposal to treat industrial wastes in municipal sewage systems (because of toxic materials), but this did not result in changes in the report. Opposition by officials from Coventry and West Warwick, Rhode Island, did lead to both the abandonment of the SENE draft recommendation for a regional sewage plant in the latter community and the writing of substitute recommendations. One town official pointed out that the problem areas in Coventry stood furthest removed from West Warwick and that the study's information about existing sewer lines appeared erroneous. Citizens also noted that the West Warwick plant had just been expanded and that residents would be unreceptive to additional efforts.[52]

Several of the meetings also addressed the water supply situations in local communities; most of the recommendations received favorable review. In a limited number of cases local citizens corrected statements in the report and offered other considerations, which the staff took into account. A major recommendation that was reassessed as a result of such exchanges was the call for the diversion of the Weweantic River to supply water for the city of New Bedford, Massachusetts. Public comments by the head of an area laboratory, which monitored the river as a matter of practice, emphasized its high level of pesticides, hence its unsuitability for water supply purposes. The staff dropped this recommendation in the final report.[53]

Though it would be possible to continue this process of identification further, the above instances serve to exemplify the impact on the study made by citizens at the public meetings. It is true that citizen responses, as in the LISS Study, were not uniform, but discernible preferences did at times emerge. In many instances, though certainly not in all, these preferences resulted in changes in the SENE planning reports.

Probably the most dramatic influence by citizens on the SENE Study occurred after the final series of public meetings but within the review period. At the May 1975 meeting in the Buzzards Bay area some local residents had criticized the study's recommendations for the expansion of the major state park in the area, the acquisition of several river islands for recreational purposes, and the expansion of local boating facilities. This opposition solidified over the summer, as evidenced in the press, in the letters and phone calls to the SENE staff, and in the circulation of a petition (reportedly signed by over a thousand residents). The residents also charged that little advance notice of the meeting had been received—a claim supported by the local weekly newspaper, which stated that it had received the notice too late for publication.[54]

In response the SENE staff held another meeting in the area that August. The staff invited about ten community leaders to discuss the recommendations with them, a format which, while reflecting the desires of the staff for a working session, was criticized locally. Actually, over two dozen residents attended the session, which focused on the environmentally fragile nature of the islands, their use as a habitat by rare wildlife, the present adequacy of the state park and of the local management of the surrounding lands, and the crowded boating conditions in the area. Subsequently, the staff announced basic changes in the recommendations, dropping entirely the plans for expansion. This case exemplifies the impact of citizens' comments on the SENE Study in its clearest form.[55]

Impact of Citizen Participants on the CRBP Study

Citizens also had a comparable effect on the planning activities and the final report of the Connecticut River Basin Program's Supplemental Flood Plain Management Study. Indeed, that citizens had an influence on the CRBP plan could hardly be termed surprising, since initiation of the Supplemental Study was a result of significant citizen involvement. As discussed above, many citizens had reacted negatively to the 1970 Comprehensive Study, prepared by a coordinating committee under the leadership of the Corps, and NERBC had created the Citizens Review Committee to help it assess the plan.[56] The criticisms raised in turn by this group, which called for a broader assessment of environmental concerns, led to NERBC's recommendation of the CRBP Study.

I will examine the influence of citizens on the CRBP Study, itself. In this case, too, the impact of advisory group members differed from those of the general public and are examined separately. Since the CRBP CAG and SAG functioned autonomously early in the planning process and later merged their activities, their influence is assessed accordingly.

Impact of the advisory group members. During its early meetings, starting in March 1973, the Citizens Advisory Group (CAG) sought to organize itself and to learn more about the study and its role in it. In particular, discussion focused on the role of the CAG in publicizing the study. Members established a Public Information Committee to work on this task. Comments at these and later meetings also emphasized the need for social impact studies as a part of the planning process. These comments, coupled with similar concerns expressed by the science advisers, encouraged the staff to hire a consultant to undertake such investigations, even though doing so had not been previously contemplated.[57]

During this period the SAG, which had begun meeting earlier than the CAG, became deeply involved in the substantive elements of the planning process. SAG quickly adopted a subcommittee system, and during early 1973 individual subcommittees and the group as a whole met with consultants and agency representatives to discuss both the tasks to be undertaken by them and the appropriate methodologies to be used. As noted by several observers, SAG criticism, directed at the early report of a consulting firm and coupled with a negative reaction by the Study Management Team, led the CRPB staff to back away from the methodologies embraced in that report.[58] At their third meeting, in April 1973, SAG responded to a draft Plan of Study, the document intended to guide the planning process. The members also began to address six broad methodological concerns posed by the CRBP staff and reformulated into questions by the SAG chairman. These were referred to the appropriate subcommittees for study. SAG forwarded a preliminary report of their findings to the Study Management Team during the next month, and work on this and related projects by the subcommittees continued.

Despite the importance of these activities, the impact of SAG on the study during this period appears limited.[59] As one staff member later wrote, most SAG responses were general, reflecting the complexity of the assignments and the fact that SAG members were volunteers with limited time to devote to the study.[60] As seen above in Professor Berger's comments, the imprecise role of SAG at this stage of the study also discouraged some participants. Consequently, the level of activity among the subcommittees was uneven. The Soil Conservation Service did ask one subcommittee to assist in the selection of a third small watershed for in-depth study. The subcommittee selected the Mill River, a choice endorsed by SAG and accepted by the agency.[61] One controversial issue which arose concerned the role SAG should play in reviewing Requests for Proposals developed by the staff. Because of potential charges of conflict of interest, the staff decided that SAG should not review the requests and that proposals would not be accepted from SAG members.[62]

In late 1973 and early 1974 comparable subcommittees of both the Citizens and Science advisory groups began their review of the study's Phase 1 documents. The similarity of their assignments led to interaction between the parallel subcommittees, which encouraged the holding of joint CAG/SAG meetings. These subcommittees and their parent bodies reviewed a variety of reports, offering in certain cases specific and detailed criticism. The CRBP staff, in turn, forwarded the comments to the appropriate public agency or consulting firm for consideration.

These reviews underscored a broad variety of methodological and environmental concerns.[63] Members were quick to point out statements which they felt could not be empirically substantiated. They also identified instances where they felt environmental concerns and nonstructural alternatives were not adequately assessed.[64] The impact on these reviews is difficult to assess, however, for there existed no direct reporting mechanism by which the planners outside the CRBP staff responded to the citizens' comments. A number of subcommittee members worked closely with certain agencies, especially those dealing with environmental matters. Several SAG and CAG members, as well as the CRBP staff, believed that some agencies and consulting firms had taken the comments of advisory group members into account in subsequent reports.[65] At best the record was uneven, varying from agency to agency and from one individual member to another. This was also true of the later review by citizens and scientists of the Phase 2 reports.

While the review process continued, the joint CAG/SAG meetings addressed a number of concerns beyond the restricted scope of the Supplemental Study. For example, the combined groups developed and sent to NERBC a list of implementation priorities for the Connecticut River.[66] At first, a joint subcommittee and then the groups as a whole reacted to a draft environmental impact statement for the Northeast Water Supply (NEWS) study, recently completed by the Army Corps of Engineers. The product of these sessions was a twenty-four-page subcommittee report, a compilation of positions rather than a consensus statement, which the groups forwarded to the CRBP staff and the Corps' Board of Engineers for Rivers and Harbors.[67] Finally, the groups also examined the need for fish ladders at a power company dam at Turners Falls, Massachusetts, in order to permit anadromous fish to return upstream to spawn. The members issued a strong statement calling upon the power company involved to build the fish ladders and upon the then Federal Power Commission, by means of its licensing powers, to ensure that this was accomplished.[68] With this resolution in hand, several members lobbied vigorously for the ladders.[69] Although the impacts of the citizen activities prove difficult to assess and lay outside the Supplemental Study, CAG/SAG activity did help to motivate NERBC, which adopted a formal position on the fish ladders and licensing procedures similar to that of the advisory groups.

After this, attention focused again on the Supplemental Study and what was to become one of its most sensitive issues, a question of methodology. At a meeting in May 1975, the advisers discussed the difference between estimates, by the Corps of Engineers and by the CRBP staff, of the economic benefits and costs of building major dams or raising local protection works (dikes and floodwalls) at key locations along the river.[70] The CAG and SAG members present explored this highly technical issue in superficial terms. Several members complained that they lacked the essential information to evaluate the assumptions underlying the competing sets of figures, but especially those of the Corps. The CRBP staff, while willing to discuss the matter at this session, had not made available their own draft paper on the subject. In addition, representatives of the Corps had declined to attend the meeting—

a decision which annoyed the advisory committee members. Nevertheless, the comments expressed by the advisers clearly favored the CRBP staff's figures, which offered a less optimistic view of the dam-building and dike-raising options. Indeed, the advisers later used the staff's calculations to criticize the Corps, an act that strained relations between that organization—which was a member of the planning team—and the CRBP office.[71] Unresolved, this matter surfaced again at the next joint meeting.

At this May meeting CAG and SAG members also reacted strongly, as discussed above, against the SENE Study's failure to qualify its recommendation for the Northfield Water Supply Project.[72] A letter to the SENE staff explained the objections; later, a SAG member met with the SENE staff and advisory groups. As already noted, changes in the SENE plan resulted. This proved to be a unique case of the citizen advisers to one study having an impact on another.

Two months later SAG and CAG members met to react to the first draft of the CRBP report. In general, they endorsed the plan, spelling out a number of specific changes which they desired— mainly the text of the summary. Several CAG and SAG comments sought to clarify the terminology of the report. The members also suggested that the staff should:

(1) encourage compatible land uses in the flood plain;
(2) emphasize local responsibility for plan implementation and state responsibility for preventing new development in the flood plain;
(3) recommend that the Corps of Engineers should use Fiscal Year 1976 funds to accelerate flood plain delineation;
(4) use their own methodology for calculating the costs and benefits of raising the dikes in major cities and present the Corps' methodologies and an explanation in the report's appendix;
(5) include education as an element of an implementation strategy; and
(6) display in the report minimum nonstructural programs.[73]

In subsequent drafts of the report, the CRBP staff gave significantly greater attention to the role of local governments in implementing the plan and the need to educate the public about the issues. However, the Study Management Team did not seriously consider the option of relegating to an appendix the Corps' cost/benefit figures for the seven dams and the local protection works. In fact, when the CAG chairman expressed this point at the July 31st SMT meeting, no planners even responded to him.[74]

At a meeting in March 1976, the advisers' discussion of the 90-day review draft of the CRBP report added little in the way of substantive comments.[75] Their focus by this time was on implementing rather than modifying the plan, although several members did attend and contribute to a subsequent SMT meeting held to discuss revisions in the draft plan. Individual members also submitted further oral and written comments directly to the staff during the 90-day review period.[76]

As for assessing the impact of these specific CAG/SAG responses to the CRBP draft documents, I believe that, at the reviewing stage, they had a relatively minor effect on the text of the plan finally approved by the Commission in December 1976.[77] Much of the CAG/SAG discussion focused on the language of the report and its readability; yet other agency and lay reviewers shared these concerns. Despite the advisory groups' objections, the final report presented both the Corps' and CRBP's cost-benefit figures. It did explicitly state, however, that the Citizens and Science advisory groups favored the latter analysis.[78]

Certain of the individual advisers' specific comments also appeared in the final report. For example, one criticism—that the section on dikes failed to mention the tendencies of such structures to thwart public access and obscure urban vistas—led to a broader discussion of such costs.[79] Similarly, complaints of excessive reliance on the four state governments (rather than a regional or national body) for implementing the plan encouraged the staff to expand its treatment of such matters.[80] NERBC also responded to the comments of certain advisers by reaffirming the role of the Citizens and Science advisory groups in basin planning in the future.[81] In general, however, the paucity of comments forthcoming from the advisory groups at these latter review stages and their limited effect on the final draft of *The River's Reach* reflected the satisfaction of most members with the basic elements of the final plan, especially its nonstructural components.

Impact of public meeting attendees and other citizen participants. The citizens who attended the CRBP's public meetings also had an input into the Supplemental Study, as did the many individuals, including some meeting attendees, who established a direct contact with the staff. In most cases their contributions to the study became increasingly more specific as the planning progressed.

As with LISS and the SENE Study, the first series of public meetings provided an opportunity to inform local residents about the CRBP Study. A major portion of the meetings was devoted to answering citizens' questions. The attendees indicated their preference for considering both a broad range of flood management alternatives and various ways of compensating local governments for the cost of resulting actions.[82] At a few meetings renewed opposition arose to major dams that had been earlier proposed by the Corps' study in 1970.

The timing of the second series of public meetings permitted citizens to react to a broad range of flood-control alternatives which the planners were in the process of formulating for their areas as well as for the basin as a whole. They did so, although with some uneasiness at times because the costs of various options had not been calculated at that point. Their inputs at these meetings, however, had an impact on the CRBP plan.

Probably the clearest message emanating from the meetings was the unacceptability of the Corps' seven-dam proposal.[83] Citizens at all the meetings, including those held in the lower basin where support for the dams would logically be the strongest, voiced opposition to that option. Massachusetts and Connecticut citizens and their local officials accepted the alternative of dike-raising as a solution to flood problems. In the draft and final reports, which followed at a much later date, the staff focused on dike-raising proposals for the urban areas in the lower portions of the basin.[84] Later, at the next and final series of meetings, they announced that the dams were "dead." Although modified by the dike-raising proposals, broad support emerged for nonstructural alternatives. The draft and final reports reflected these concerns.

The attendees at several meetings also reacted to other alternative strategies under consideration. For example, citizens at the Brattleboro, Vermont, meeting spoke against several alternatives involving the construction of dams, especially on one site constituting prime farm land.[85] Later, the 90-day review draft plan noted these comments and did not recommend the dams objected to earlier by the area residents.[86] Later also the Study Management Team considered alternatives suggested by citizens at several local meetings. At the request of a local official, the Corps of Engineers considered a dredging project in one flood-prone area but later termed it economically unfeasible.[87] Finally, there was much criticism, particularly in northern areas, of federal intervention in any form regardless of the alternative recommended. This attitude influenced the CRBP staff's decision not to recommend a special "Section 73" study, designed to implement federal cost sharing for nonstructural flood plain management under P.L. 93-251, for the Passumpsic watershed in Northeastern Vermont.[88]

Citizens attending the third round of public meetings and those writing directly to the staff generally endorsed the regional recommendations of the draft CRBP report and the non- and minimal-structural thrust of the plan. More specific comments focused primarily on the particular recommendations of the study for given local areas. As in LISS and the SENE Study, some of these citizen inputs led directly to changes in the text of the final report; others did not.

For example, the CRBP plan called for further study of dike-raising in three major cities along the lower reaches of the river, but not in two others. Officials and citizens from one of the latter two cities—Chicopee, Massachusetts—expressed a strong desire, both at one meeting and in later letters to the staff, for further investigations in their community.[89] The final report was modified to leave open such a possibility, under specified conditions. In contrast, the staff did not accept arguments by the St. Johnsbury, Vermont, Chamber of Commerce for channel work in their area.[90] Similarly, faced with comments for and against its recommendation that certain homes and businesses in the Claremont, New Hampshire, and St. Johnsbury areas should be immediately relocated, the staff continued to prefer that action.[91] Finally, still other comments reinforced what the advisers had said earlier about more clearly defining the responsibilities of local and other governments in carrying out the plan and in this way affected the final report.

In general, then, the meeting attendees and other citizens who expressed their opinions about the Supplemental Study at various stages of the planning process had an impact on the final CRBP report. One can make the same point with regard to the Citizens and Science advisory groups. Difficulty in identifying more profound impacts than those discussed above may be primarily traced to the extent to which those who participated were satisfied with the resulting plan. To a lesser extent staff members did not act on some inputs directed at local problems which were inconsistent with the broadly supported regional strategies incorporated in the report.

An Overview

In the Long Island Sound Study, the Southeastern New England Study, and the Connecticut River Basin Program's Supplemental Study, the public participants had an identifiable impact on the planning processes and the draft and final planning reports. For the public meeting attendees, these impacts occurred later in the studies, especially as they reacted to the draft planning reports. With regard to the advisory group members, these impacts were distributed throughout the course of the studies but seemed greater when the members performed specific tasks, like formulating statements of goals or reviewing planning documents.[92]

Moreover, although the effects of citizen participation varied from study to study, their resemblance is striking. This similarity makes it possible to examine collectively the nature of citizen comments and opinions on LISS, SENE, and CRBP. When one does so, one finds a variety of ways in which the citizens influenced the three studies.

First, citizens supplemented the knowledge of the regional planners, particularly with regard to local affairs. Given the broad geographical scope of the studies and other constraints placed upon the planners, the planning staffs could not be informed about particular conditions and problems in many local communities in their planning areas. In a variety of cases, local residents, more aware of such concerns, brought forth data which the staffs had not considered.

This new information on numerous occasions led the staffs to change their recommendations. For example, new information about pesticide levels in the Weweantic River caused SENE to drop its recommendation for diverting that river for water supply purposes. This type of supplemental information also seemed particularly important in shaping the recreational proposals in SENE and LISS. Many citizens in the latter study specifically questioned the knowledge of the Sound possessed by the members of the recreational work group.[93] Public participants in a limited number of cases also corrected erroneous factual statements about local conditions which appeared in various planning documents.

From the perspective of the staff members, however, several problems arose in their use of this supplemental information. The accuracy of the information had to be judged. In some cases the "facts" presented by local residents appeared rather to be statements of preference, with weak empirical referents. Also, in some cases the data appeared accurate, though not significant enough in the planners' estimation to warrant a change in the study recommendations. The degree to which the staff utilized the supplemental information provided by citizens depended upon the planners' judgments concerning its accuracy and its importance. They discarded information that failed to meet these tests.

Secondly, public participants influenced the studies by altering the use of both methodologies and planning reports by NERBC personnel. The science advisers, by virtue of their training, were attuned to viewing methodologies and their underlying assumptions with a critical eye. In many instances, such as with questions of growth, the citizen advisers and the public meeting attendees proved no less capable. The criticism by one CAC member of techniques used in the LISS boating inventory is an example of this type of influence. In general the methodological criticism offered by public participants caused the staff to reconsider assumptions, to modify information-gathering and evaluative techniques, and to use agency or consultant reports in ways different from those originally intended. This was a selective process, however, and the impact of citizens and scientists on methodological concerns varied with the assessment of their arguments by the NERBC staffs as well as by other planners associated with the studies.

Thirdly, public participants encouraged a broad consideration of both value questions and alternative solutions. On numerous occasions citizens raised additional value-laden considerations for the planners to take into account. The advisory group members of the CRBP Study, for example, urged the staff to consider all of the environmental consequences of their proposals. Here, too, the staff had to judge whether the values were appropriate and sufficiently broad-based to warrant inclusion in the studies. With regard to growth, transportation, and water supply, as examples, the advisory committees of LISS consistently viewed the study in a broader scope than did the staff itself. This forced the staff not only to define more sharply the boundaries of the study, but also to consider at least briefly the relationship of their plans to more general problems. In similar fashion, public participants pressed the staffs to explore a multitude of alternative solutions.

Fourthly, public participants directed staff attention to current problems in the study areas. As in the case of the bridge over the Sound, citizens, particularly members of the advisory groups, encouraged the staffs to take positions on issues of local importance. Such staff involvement served to give the staffs a sense of urgency, to improve relations with the advisory groups, and to generate publicity for the studies, hence, potentially increasing public awareness of the planning programs. In the extreme, however, such activities may potentially involve study personnel in fighting a series of brush fires and detract from the planning effort. They could also bring the studies into conflict with other planning organizations or other governmental units. A balanced approach is required.

Finally, citizen involvement in the studies served to make the final plans more acceptable to community leaders and others who participated in the process. In many instances the three staffs changed proposed recommendations to which participating citizens had strenuously objected. This was true in LISS with regard to the salt-water fishing license and in SENE with regard to the proposals for the development of both recreational facilities in the Buzzards Bay area and an expanded sewage treatment plant in West Warwick, Rhode Island. In other cases, when the staffs deemed it necessary they stood firmly behind their recommendations, at times offering additional explanations. Despite these latter occasions, however, it seems that the overall plans, as revised to reflect public comments, were more acceptable to citizens with an active interest in water resources usage than they would otherwise have been. Presumably, citizen participation made later implementation of the plans more likely.

In summary, public participation in the three NERBC planning programs fulfilled the expectations expressed earlier in the studies and in the related literature. The public participants had an impact on the planning process by supplementing the factual knowledge of the planners, by affecting their use of planning methodologies and reports, by stressing the need to address questions of values, by focusing the planners' attention on current problems, and by helping to evolve politically acceptable plans. The records of LISS, SENE, and CRBP suggest that public participants can have an important influence on regional planning. The controlling factor is the degree to which the administrators accept and incorporate citizen comments in the plans. The implications of this for the accountability of administrators is examined in the next chapter.

CHAPTER FIVE

Accountability in the New England River Basins Commission Studies

It is clear that the staffs of the Long Island Sound Study, the Southeastern New England Study, and the Connecticut River Basin Program made extensive efforts to integrate citizens into their regional (Level B) planning investigations, even though the mechanisms to achieve that goal were less than ideal. Most observers and the citizen participants themselves shared this assessment.[1] Moreover, a comparative examination reveals that the scope of the participation programs undertaken by NERBC staffs generally exceeded those of similar programs established by other river basins commissions.[2] Did the public participation programs in the studies result, then, in citizen control of the NERBC staff members?

Many citizens took advantage of these participation programs and made an identifiable impact on the three planning processes and their resulting plans, but the findings indicate that participation did not prove to be a totally satisfactory strategy for holding LISS, SENE, and CRBP planners accountable. Control by citizens simply did not occur.

The chief reason appears to be that citizens performed only an advisory role. They had no final controls (comparable to elections) over the planning personnel or the planning decisions, and the NERBC resisted any effort by citizens to assume such powers. For example, early in LISS the request of CAC members to make their chairman a "voting member" (along with the agency representatives) of the study's Coordinating Committee was dismissed.[3] The CAC members, their leaders, or other citizen participants in the three studies never enjoyed such voting or decision-making privileges, nor did the Commission grant citizen participants control over any functional part of the process. Thus LISS, SENE, and CRBP planners were not answerable directly to the citizen participants for the manner in which they carried out their responsibilities. The citizens had influence—their complaints, along with other factors, nearly led to the replacement of one study manager—yet the administrators made all planning decisions, and acted upon citizen requests only at their own discretion.[4] One may ask, then, to what extent public participation at least enhanced the accountability of the planners who were responsible for these regional investigations.

No simple answer to that question is possible. The influence that citizens exerted was extremely complex.

Limits of Accountability

Many characteristics of the citizen involvement limited the degree to which it strengthened administrative accountability. Five of the chief reasons are: (1) the limited degree to which participants were representative; (2) structural impediments in the planning and participation programs; (3) unclear definitions of roles assigned to participants; (4) the timing of citizen involvement; and (5) the parochial attitudes and low informational levels of many of the participants.

(1) *The problem of representativeness.* The rationale for public participation suggests that involvement will increase the control of the general citizenry over administrative policy-makers. It seems doubtful in many respects, however, that the citizens involved in the three studies—the advisory committee members, as well as those attending the meetings—adequately represented the general public. This issue of representation aroused considerable debate through the course of the planning investigations themselves. In particular, it continually troubled members of the citizens advisory committees and the NERBC staffs, neither of whom ever completely resolved the matter.[5] Though important, such assessments of how representative participants are prove hard to make,

primarily because "representativeness" is an elusive concept that can be evaluated by various standards. As Pitkin asserts, the representativeness of a public official may be judged by the extent to which that person (1) possesses binding authority; (2) answers to the people being served; (3) mirrors the characteristics of the represented; (4) symbolically stands for the people; and (5) deliberately acts on behalf of the interests of the other citizens.[6] Any statement about the representativeness of our citizen participants must take these criteria into account.

In applying the criteria to LISS, SENE, and CRBP, one finds that in some ways the citizen participants did represent a larger public. First, numerous participants held elected or appointed office at the local or regional level. According to the questionnaire, 31.6 percent of the people attending the final meetings fell into this group, and 45.6 percent in the SENE Study. Members of the advisory committees also, in some cases, held such positions. Presumably, then, the comments of citizens/officials reflected the interests and preferences of their politically active constituents and in that limited way were representative.

Secondly, that sixteen of the LISS and twenty-four of the CRBP citizens advisory committee members had been appointed by their respective governors led some of these participants to feel that they represented their governors and, in turn, the electorate of their states. In fact several members of the CRBP CAG espoused this view.[7] With regard to the two-tiered advisory structure of the SENE Study, it can also be argued that CAC members selected at the public meetings (BAC meetings) represented primarily the people present at those sessions and only secondarily the other residents of the areas.

Thirdly, in CRBP far more than in LISS and SENE, the staff at times encouraged citizen advisers to ensure that "all interests" in the Basin were taken into account.[8] Because the staff foresaw that environmental groups would be more inclined than other interests to participate actively in the Supplemental Study, it sought to obligate the CAG members to take a broad view on upcoming planning matters "to help keep the door open to other considerations."[9] It also stressed the role of the CAG in transmitting information about the study to other potentially affected parties.

Even in those respects, however, the representative qualities of the citizen participants proved to be limited. There is no indication that the citizen participants, including most advisory group members, systematically sought to represent "all interests," or the general public. In contrast, Shanley's research shows that the members of the LISS CAC had many different views about whom or what they represented, whether themselves, local citizens, the members of a particular interest group to which they belonged, a body of knowledge, a broader range of people, or some combination thereof.[10] This appeared to be the case with the SENE and CRBP CAC's also. Ertel in her survey of citizen advisers found that only 50 percent from CRBP, 45 percent from LISS, and 33 percent from SENE considered their groups representative.[11]

Moreover, both NERBC personnel, in guiding the CAC selection process, and governors, in making the LISS and CRBP appointments, failed to emphasize and develop the notion of representativeness. Only a very few LISS and CRBP advisory committee members reported seeking guidance from their governors or from other public officials.[12] In the SENE Study the advisory committee members did not retain direct links to the citizens who selected them because, as noted, the BAC's never really functioned as cohesive groups. Such a formal linkage between the CAC and a broader public did not exist in LISS and CRBP. The representation provided by the local and regional officials participating in the studies may similarly be questioned, for many were not there in an official capacity, and whom they were speaking for remains uncertain.

More importantly, the majority of the citizens participating in the three studies and many of the advisory committee members were not public officials or gubernatorial appointees and were clearly not representing a larger public by virtue of either their status or their appointment.[13] Ron Nelson, the LISS Public Participation Coordinator, has observed specifically that public officials were not well integrated into LISS.[14] Whom most participants represented, then, is uncertain.

An examination of the demographic characteristics and substantive interests of the citizens involved makes it even clearer that they were not representative of the public at large. Participants had characteristics, like higher income and educational levels, and special interests, like environmental concerns, which distinguished them from most others in their regions. Advisory committee members were set apart further by the self-selection process. Even initially, however, the elaborate appointment mechanisms presented problems to the staffs as they sought to create balanced groups. In LISS and CRBP, where the governors made a substantial number of appointments independent of one another and NERBC, the staffs found it impossible to control the composition of those groups. Delli Priscoli argues that the careful screening of appointees to the citizens advisory committees led to the selection of members who were atypically low risks in terms of challenging the planners.[15]

In a variety of instances, these distinctive characteristics and interests colored the manner in which the participants defined problems and the recommendations they offered. For example, one staff member stated that the LISS CAC displayed a disproportionate interest in boating problems, a tendency he traced to the atypical number of boat-owners in the group. Similarly, he observed that only individuals with above-average wealth could afford to view the Sound primarily as an "ecological unit," a view shared by many CAC members and other participants at the public meetings.[16] Less affluent individuals, he predicted, would be less concerned with boats and the environment than with swimming and jobs.[17] Admittedly, such demographic characteristics and interests do not uniformly affect political behavior, and it can be argued that highly educated people are quite capable of and perhaps inclined toward considering the needs of others in society. Since few procedures or guidelines for encouraging this broader view existed in these studies, however, and especially in LISS and SENE, it is difficult to see how many participants could be representative in this paternalistic sense. Clearly, in terms of significant demographic characteristics, such as income, age, race, and education, the citizen participants did not and could not express the wishes of the entire population of a region. Even when LISS, SENE, and CRBP planners responded to the suggestions of advisory committee members and other participants, they were not necessarily responding to the preferences of citizens as a whole.

(2) *The problem of structure.* The decision-making structures of both the three planning investigations and the three participation programs also limited the extent to which public participation in the studies enhanced bureaucratic accountability. In assessing this limitation, two points should be recalled. First, while the LISS, SENE, and CRBP staffs coordinated their respective studies, the decision-making authority was diffused in these Level B investigations. Various federal agencies with separate budgets produced sections of each plan. In addition, NERBC, the parent organization, had to approve all final planning documents. Secondly, the citizen participants formally served as advisers to the separate LISS, SENE, and CRBP planning staffs rather than to the agencies associated with the studies, or to the Commission itself.

Because of the structure of the public participation programs, the citizens, in interacting primarily with one of the regional staffs, did not frequently become involved in a give-and-take with many of the principal actors in the investigations. The LISS, SENE, and CRBP staffs did on occasion use the opinions expressed by citizen participants as levers in negotiating with other planners, and a few members of other agencies did speak at various advisory committee meetings, but regular and meaningful involvement in the public meetings by non-NERBC planners associated with the studies occurred only in the CRBP Supplemental Study. In turn, citizen participation in the work groups, where the planners made many of the substantive planning decisions, was very limited as well as sporadic. When advisory group members participated in those sessions, they did so at a disadvantage because they had not been closely informed of the agencies' activities. As noted by one LISS CAC member: "There was unremitting frustration on the part of many of the CAC members who found the agencies unprepared to accept the citizens in a partnership on the work groups."[18] Perhaps part of the reason for this unpreparedness was that the agencies retained their own traditional constituencies.

The citizen participants and the Boston-based staff of the Commission itself maintained only limited contact. This was particularly true of the CRBP Study; closer, though still limited, contact was made in the SENE Study, the office of which was in the same city (Boston) as that of NERBC. In general, the influence the citizens exerted in these studies was over only one of several groups of planners responsible for the completion of each project. Citizen participation therefore failed to increase the accountability of the other associated federal administrators.

Furthermore, the decision-making structure of these Level B studies impeded the efforts of citizen participants. The NERBC chairman asserted that the three staffs were deprived of the "essential ingredient of good management—clear authority and a reasonable degree of control over study resources."[19] This situation posed two particular problems: it left the citizens uncertain of the powers of the three staffs and what they could expect them to perform, and when the planners sought to be responsive to the citizen participants, structural and financial constraints limited their ability to act.

Finally, the very nature of the NERBC hampered bureaucratic accountability. As a recently established planning organization, with limited funds and a small staff, the Commission lacked recognition by the public at large. This made it more difficult for the three staffs to obtain news coverage and to attract representative citizens to their public events. In part, because internal and external constraints limited efforts to publicize the studies, many of the citizen participants, especially those attending the public meetings, did not have a basic familiarity with the agency that they sought to influence. In summary, the ways in which both the studies themselves and their public participation programs were structured made it difficult for citizens to influence the planning decisions made and to hold accountable the various planners involved.

(3) *The problem of the citizens' role.* Inconsistencies in and confusion over the advisory role played by citizens restricted the efforts to enhance accountability. These inconsistencies stemmed from the fact that in practice the citizens played dual roles in the studies and operated under different sets of standards and expectations. Several specific problems may be identified.

First, the citizens played a dual role as both insiders and outsiders. At times the participants functioned outside of the planning process as seemingly neutral observers, attempting to provide a critical review of the plans; at other times they operated inside the process, enmeshed in the studies.[20] Although many participants remained aloof from the planning, in part because of the structural detachment of the participation programs, others did not. Some participants, especially the advisory committee members, became highly integrated into and closely identified with the process. Given such ties, whether the citizens could still provide an objective review of the proceedings is an interesting yet unresolved question. Certainly many of the advisers observed by me appeared to retain their independence and objectivity, but the possibility of subtle cooptation remains.

Secondly, the three staffs developed and used formal devices for generating citizen advice, and in this sense placed numerous demands upon the citizens; yet they did not obligate themselves in any way to follow that advice.[21] For example, the staffs asked advisory committee members to follow the extensive procedural guidelines regarding voting on committee business, attendance at meetings, and speaking about committee business. In particular, the procedures called for citizens and science advisory committees to submit advice to the staffs in the form of recommendations adopted by majority vote on given resolutions. However, the staffs did not necessarily act on these advisory recommendations.

At the staff level there were a few systematic procedures for evaluating the advice of participants and reporting the results back to the citizens. The CRBP staff made some gains in this direction by organizing citizen comments into special publications, such as *The Local Perspectives Report*.[22] Rather than issuing simply minutes or summaries of the CAG meetings, the staff also circulated what it called "reports," which sought to interpret and at times respond to citizen comments.[23] The LISS and SENE staffs did not use such a systematic approach except at the very end of their studies, when, like CRBP, they summarized the comments made at the final series of public meetings and stated their reaction to them.[24]

Viewing this formalism on one hand, yet lack of commitment on the other, Delli Priscoli found it hard to see the benefits for some groups in submitting to such procedures.[25] Some incentive undoubtedly lay in greater access to the study information, yet this dualism probably discouraged some individuals or groups from using these mechanisms to participate.[26] Delli Priscoli also noted that these conditions made it likely that participants would become frustrated and that the potential for "capturing new and interesting views" would not be maximized.[27] Rather impressionistic evidence suggests that the former may have caused some of the advisory committee resignations.[28] In general, the staffs' lack of both systematic response to citizen comments and commitment to use the advice in itself reduced the impact of the participants on the studies. Coupled with the formality of the advisers' procedures, these factors discouraged certain individuals from participating, thereby reducing citizen input into the studies.

Thirdly, the LISS, SENE, and CRBP staffs viewed the citizen participants alternately as leaders of key groups, as experts, and as members of the public at large.[29] Indeed, some participants did seem to represent all three categories, although to varying degrees. Given these varying perceptions of the participants, however, the staffs found it difficult to judge the legitimacy of the advice offered them, and this uncertainty also limited the impact of citizen comments.

Together, these various inconsistencies and doubts with regard to the advisory role of participants raised questions in the three staffs about the appropriateness of using the participants' recommendations and served to limit the impact of this advice on the studies. They also tended to discourage some citizens from participating in the planning process, a tendency that not only further reduced citizen inputs, but also diminished the representative quality of the participants.

(4) *Problems of timing.* Problems associated with the timing of citizen participation in the studies similarly limited accountability. In assessing these effects, it is important to note that participation occurred within a specific time frame, and within that period it took place at well defined stages. Both sets of conditions diminished bureaucratic accountability.

As to the general timing of their involvement in the planning processes, citizens participated in the three studies from very late in the writing of the plans of study until the staffs had produced the final drafts of the plans.[30] This timing posed two particular problems.

First, the citizen advisers did not participate early in the pre-authorization planning processes, when the administrators established broad frameworks for the Level B investigations. Although in both LISS and SENE interim CAC's counseled the staffs on the structure of the envisaged public participation programs, these citizens had little identifiable impact on the remainder of the two plans of study.[31] Furthermore, once all three studies formally began, delays in the appointment of the regular members of citizens advisory committees limited their involvement in the early planning activities. In the LISS and CRBP studies, such delays can be attributed to the complexity of the appointment processes and the lack of prompt responses from various governors; in SENE such delays stemmed from both the unique two-tiered advisory structure and the staff's slowness in establishing the BAC's, which were responsible for selecting many of the members of the regional CAC. This overall situation served to reduce citizen influence in the early planning stages of all three studies.

Secondly, public involvement in two of the three studies ended abruptly as the staffs produced the final plans. Only in CRBP, where the advisers were attached to an ongoing program and where subsequent planning activities (Section 73 studies) began immediately, did the Citizens and Science advisory groups continue to function. NERBC closed the LISS and SENE offices and dissolved their staffs; the advisory committees and the other aspects of their public participation programs ceased to act. These latter advisory committee members lost the prerogatives associated with their formal status as advisers; the limited funding of their expenses incurred in advising the staffs ended. Given these changes, citizens in the Long Island Sound and Southeastern New England areas could not readily participate in subsequent decisions concerning the plans, including those related to implementation. Citizen influence with respect to the LISS and SENE plans and the respective planners waned.

Moreover, as Ortolano indicates is true of most water resources planning efforts, citizen involvement in LISS, SENE, and CRBP occurred at well-defined stages.[32] Apart from the recommendations of advisory group members, the staff received other public inputs primarily at or soon after each series of public meetings, sessions that were held, roughly speaking, at yearly intervals in each study. Participation at such fixed intervals is not ideally suited for water resources planning. Indeed, Sax observes that planning is continuous over years, "rarely having clearly definable points at which critical decisions are made."[33] To the extent that many interested and involved citizens did not participate continuously in the studies, therefore, their influence over decisions made by staff members was limited.

Citizens actively participated in each study for a fixed period of time, which began too late and—in LISS and SENE—ended too early, and their involvement within this period often occurred at well defined stages—all of which restricted the participants' influence over the NERBC and other planners. These factors too limited the ability of citizens to hold planners responsible for their actions.

(5) *Problems of information and attitudes.* Finally, the survey responses revealed still other problems associated with public participation. The first concerned the relative lack of knowledge about the studies which characterized the participants. Of the citizens attending the last round of public meetings, only one third had attended previous LISS, SENE, or CRBP public meetings. Just under a quarter (23.9 percent) had attended another group meeting at which the plans had been discussed. Fewer than half (42.5 percent) reported reading about the study in a newspaper, and, as noted, coverage often proved both superficial and incomplete. This figure was high among LISS respondents (61.3 percent) but particularly low among SENE respondents (20.8 percent).

Although many citizens received a summary of the plan for their region prior to attending meetings, only one third had read the summary in entirety. Another third had read part of it, although how much of it they examined is unknown. The remaining third had not reviewed the summary at all. Percentages of discussions between citizens and either advisory committee members or staff members are similar: just over a fifth of the citizens had discussed the plan with an advisory committee member; 23.2 percent had discussed it with a staff member. Thus when the SENE and

CRBP meeting-goers were asked, "Do you feel that you know enough about the study to be able to offer comments at tonight's meeting?" about half answered negatively (SENE 52.7 percent and CRBP 44.6 percent).[34]

In assessing these figures, one must keep in mind that they are not mutually exclusive. Indeed, it seems likely that citizens who were informed about the study at earlier meetings or by newspaper were those who communicated with the staffs and the advisory committee members. These figures do suggest that a group —probably a minority—within the total number of meeting attendees was comparatively active and informed, but that a significant number apparently possessed little knowledge of the substance of the plans. Compared to the planners, many citizens attending the public meetings were at an informational disadvantage, and this situation limited their ability to influence the plans and to hold planners accountable. It also seems reasonable to infer that the informed group of meeting attendees, like the generally well informed members of the advisory committees, had an influence on the studies greater than their numbers would suggest.

Secondly, though numerous individuals expressed an interest in broad environmental issues, others demonstrated their interest in how the studies' recommendations would affect their community or their private property. This tendency was especially strong in CRBP meetings, where citizens realized the potential impact of the flood control recommendations on their property and its value.[35] About a fifth of them at CRBP meetings (20.6 percent) asserted that their primary concern was for private property. Similarly, the questionnaire responses reflected citizen preferences for a strong local role in water resources planning.

This local orientation raises serious questions about the appropriateness of citizen involvement in Level B planning efforts. A fundamental tension developed as the staffs, charged with taking a regional focus, found many citizens reluctant to think in such terms. In particular, citizens balked at placing in their communities what the staffs deemed to be facilities needed by the region (such as for recreation, power generation, or waste disposal). Innumerable debates outside of the studies have revealed a similar tension. Were the planners to follow such expressed local preferences, few regional facilities would be built.

If the citizens' lack of adequate information about the studies limited their influence on the staffs, the extent to which public meetings generated comments addressed to local concerns at the expense of regional ones revealed a basic problem in seeking to hold regional planners accountable to citizen participants. This posed an added dilemma for the LISS, SENE, and CRBP public participation coordinators, who correctly perceived that one way to maximize turnout at the meetings was to stress the impact of the plans on the surrounding localities, yet who knew also that the citizens so attracted would be critical of the distinctly regional features of the studies.[36]

To summarize, a variety of characteristics of LISS, SENE, and CRBP and of citizen involvement in them limited the ability of public participation to serve as a mechanism for enhancing bureaucratic accountability. The citizens who actually participated did not represent the public at large either demographically or in terms of their method of selection. The structure both of the participation programs, which facilitated citizen contact with only the core NERBC staffs and not the other associated planners, and of the planning processes, which circumscribed the powers of the LISS, SENE, and CRBP staffs, reduced citizen influence. Inconsistencies in the role played by the citizens did the same, while compounding the problem of representativeness by discouraging some individuals from participating. The timing of public involvement, which occurred at well defined stages within a period starting belatedly and ending abruptly, also restricted citizen influence. For these reasons, citizens found it difficult to influence the planning activities.

Moreover, the participants' lack of information about the studies and their local orientation lead one to question the value and legitimacy of their advice (as does their unrepresentative nature). Yet the role of citizens advisory group members as intermediaries between LISS, SENE, and CRBP planners and less interested, but affected interests should not be downplayed. It is difficult to assess how well the CAC members in these studies performed this com munications function, but to the extent that they were successful, one should place somewhat less emphasis on their unrepresentative qualities.[37]

Enhancement of Accountability

Citizen participation proved an imperfect means for holding planners and other administrators involved in LISS, SENE, and CRBP answerable to the public at large for their activities. This general finding is hardly surprising, for many writers have found flaws in other methods of providing accountability. Nevertheless, the participating citizens did have an identifiable impact on the formulation of plans. In the light of this influence, it is appropriate to assess the general effects of their involvement. Given the problems and imperfections just considered, did public participation enhance or degrade the accountability of these planners? In pursuing answers to these questions, the following discussion examines both the direct effects of participation on bureaucratic accountability and its effects on other methods for controlling administrators.

The direct effects on accountability. The problem to be faced here is the lack of accepted standards by which to evaluate such impacts. Hanchey and others have suggested that observers should focus on certain critical questions. Is the information provided by citizens useful? Are critical issues raised by this process?[38] These researchers maintain that public participation should be judged less by the number of citizens involved or, perhaps, their demographic characteristics and more by what participation achieves in terms of policy results.[39] This focus, as I have affirmed above, makes eminent sense in that it offers a more policy-oriented, less legalistic, approach to the subject of administrative accountability, one in keeping with the significant role that bureaucrats play in public policy-making.

When one adopts such a policy orientation, questions surface which can be used appropriately to guide further inquiry. Did citizen involvement in the studies cause the planners to use their powers and their limited resources to serve the interests of the citizenry in the best way possible? Did more responsible planning documents result? A useful way of addressing these questions is by utilizing the three evaluative criteria discussed earlier: effectiveness, responsiveness, and lawfulness. In applying these criteria to the effects of citizen participation in the LISS, SENE, and CRBP Studies, I have found that citizen participation had a positive influence on the three planning processes and, in turn, on bureaucratic accountability.

First, in terms of effectiveness, citizen involvement had few negative impacts on the studies. The cost of such participation in dollars and time remained a relatively small portion of the total money spent and the time invested over the course of the three studies. The funds expended on the salaries of the public participation coordinators and the participation activities amounted to about 2 to 3 percent of the total costs of the projects.[40] Citizen-caused mental discomforts to staff members reached appreciable levels only in LISS, and even there tensions abated over time. Moreover, in studies often beset by delays, very few delays can be attributed primarily to citizen participation.

In turn, the public participants helped to produce more effective (more technically sound) final plans than would have resulted without such inputs. Citizens usefully supplemented the knowledge of planners about local conditions. At times they corrected errors resulting from a lack of information regarding, for example, the suitability of certain areas for particular kinds of recreational usage. Participants also assisted the staffs in addressing various methodological questions, redressing on occasion flaws in the reasoning, as during the initial LISS boating inventories. The role of the LISS CAC in raising the issue of access to the Sound demonstrates that participants also aided the staffs in identifying goals and problems.[41] Finally, in numerous instances citizens suggested alternative means to solving water-related problems, which because of their means-end efficiency were adopted by LISS, SENE, and CRBP. When the staffs acceded to citizen recommendations, it was usually because of the merits of the arguments rather than for reasons of political expediency.[42]

Secondly, despite the varied problems of representativeness, citizen participation in the studies helped to produce plans more responsive to the needs and preferences of the general public than would have otherwise been the case. The advisers, although middle and upper class in their life styles and values, expanded the value-base underpinning of LISS, SENE, and CRBP.[43] As Delli Priscoli observes, "it is hard to ascertain precisely where and in what direction" citizen participation broadens the value-base of planning investigations.[44] Yet one can identify at least two distinct perspectives contributed by citizens. They broadened the value-base in the direction of environmental concerns. This stands as no mean achievement in water resources planning, where many observers have long deplored the lack of attention to such concerns. In large part the CRBP Supplemental Study had been undertaken because the earlier Comprehensive Study of the Connecticut River had given scant attention to such matters. Citizens helped to correct this discrepancy in the second effort. Overall, in stressing environmental values, for example, they expressed an important concern which might otherwise have received little attention.

Localism was a second and broadly shared perspective added by citizens. City and town officials and others, for example, expressed a strong concern for local self-government. This concern tempered recommendations by the staffs for state or national management of water resources in the study areas. Although the emphasis on "home rule" posed problems for the very concept of regional planning, it must be acknowledged that it is prevalent in New England.[45] Any plan that ignored this tradition would encounter resistance during its implementation stages.

Because it is often difficult to distinguish between public and private concerns, the breadth of other perspectives added by participants is difficult to assess.[46] For example, numerous individuals at the public meetings expressed a concern for their property rights and property values as they might be affected by recommendations of the studies. To some extent these comments reflected private concerns for individual pieces of property, but they also reflected a more generalized, more public concern for protection of private property as a principle.

Finally, the additional perspectives provided by the citizens seemed more clearly directed to a relatively narrow segment of the populations of the three study regions. In these cases, however, the planners recognized the limited nature of such claims and, exercising their prerogative, chose not to follow such advice. Thus in general citizen participation expanded the value-base of LISS, SENE, and CRBP, and the addition of different perspectives served as a salutary influence on the studies, increasing both the responsiveness and the effectiveness of the planners.

Public participation had little overt impact on the lawfulness (the legal and "due process" aspects) of the final plans. That citizens were involved in the planning, probably helped to ensure that individual rights potentially affected by the plan received due consideration. We may conclude that citizen participation aided in the formulation of responsible final plans. It increased both the capability of these plans for responding to water-related problems affecting the general public and the likelihood that they would do so, taking into account a broader range of values. In this sense, public participation increased the accountability of the planners charged with carrying out the studies.

The effects on alternate means of providing accountability. Citizen participation also enhanced administrative accountability by complementing several of the alternate methods for controlling administrators. Because citizens had an advisory role, they did not automatically detract from the accountability of the planners to the President (who appointed the NERBC chairman), his appointee (the chairman), the Congress, the courts, or fellow professionals. Instead, the creation of a body of citizens, who in some cases were well informed about the studies and in others were at least interested in them, served to strengthen these other channels of accountability.

First, when distressed about various aspects of the studies, the citizen participants contacted various congressmen or state legislators. This occurred early in LISS, for example, when progress was slow. These citizen-initiated contacts tended to increase the lawmakers' knowledge of and interest in LISS, SENE, and CRBP. That, in turn, increased oversight of these planning activities exercised by the elected officials.

Secondly, LISS, SENE, and CRBP science advisers, as well as other professionals among the citizen advisers and the meeting attendees, had an impact on three final plans. Singly and collectively, these individuals displayed a formidable range of professional qualifications and utilized them in advising the respective staffs. The influence they exerted increased the accountability of LISS,

SENE, and CRBP planners to fellow professionals, thereby enhancing this method for providing control over these administrators.

Citizen participation in these cases did not lead to citizen appeals to the courts or the President. In one other way, however, it did enhance accountability. In a limited fashion, public involvement in the studies augmented the coordinating powers of the three staffs with regard to the federal line agencies.[47] Citizen opinions became at times a lever used by the LISS, SENE, and CRBP staffs to move the members of the work groups in certain policy directions. By increasing the power of the core staffs, citizen participation tended to increase the efficiency of decentralized decision-making structures and resulted in the writing of more coherent and effective plans. That also increased the answerability of the planners to the public by making it easier to fix responsibility for given planning decisions.

Overall, citizen participation enhanced bureaucratic accountability in several ways. Local citizen input, despite the problems identified earlier, improved both the effectiveness and the responsiveness of the planning recommendations, leading to the development of responsible water resources plans. It did so in part by providing information about local problems and the suitability of staff proposals and by adding new perspectives to the undertakings. Furthermore, citizen involvement complemented other means of enhancing accountability by interesting and involving both legislators and fellow professionals in the planning processes. It also helped to increase the core staffs' leadership role, resulting in better coordinated planning efforts. Citizen participation, while an imperfect mechanism, increased administrative accountability in LISS, SENE, and CRBP.

Improving Accountability in Level B Studies

One question remains: can the level of accountability provided by citizen participation in these studies be improved? The answer is yes. Given the characteristics that limited citizen involvement, one can identify numerous ways in which LISS, SENE, and CRBP public participation programs could have been improved so as to enhance accountability. These methods may, with caution, be appropriately applied to participation programs in similar Level B investigations undertaken in the future by NERBC or its counterparts in other regions, in order to make their planners more answerable to the general public.

Increasing representativeness. In order to reduce the problem of a lack of representativeness, which limited administrative accountability in the studies, several changes seem in order. First, there existed in the studies a need to improve turnout at the public meetings, so as to ensure a broader range of participating individuals. In a few instances during the third round of LISS and CRBP meetings, inclement weather and the staffs' reluctance to reschedule events contributed to the low turnout. Another problem lay in the basic inadequacy of the notice given to citizens about the meetings. Because of the uneven newspaper coverage, planning staffs should, in future efforts, press for greater free coverage of the meeting announcements prior to the sessions. The CRBP staff's aggressive approach to radio and television might well be emulated by others in this regard. The staffs should also utilize paid advertising to publicize the meetings, something not done in these cases but which in retrospect seems necessary. In particular, this approach would have helped to bolster SENE's low attendance in its Rhode Island meetings.

Other related changes also seem desirable. The absence of minority-group representation in all three studies indicates that Level B staffs should more systematically strive to involve such individuals. This necessitates more reliance on direct personal contact with minority leaders than is found in the studies. Direct mailings will not suffice. Certain staff members tried to tailor news releases to interest minority readers, but these efforts were not systematic. Pressures of time may delimit such possibilities, but should not inhibit them.[48]

In addition, more meaningful and direct use of advisory committee members as links to their communities seems appropriate. The three staffs were overly hesitant to use advisory committee members as speakers at, or as sponsors of, small group meetings.[49] Overall, more attention should be given to the advisers' serving as a link between the planners and the public at large. As noted, the extent to which CAC members function in such a capacity rather than as direct advisers causes somewhat less significance to be attached to their unrepresentative qualities. Delli Priscoli also observes that such studies should seek to involve more social scientists in the public participation programs, since these individuals can help in collecting and interpreting data about the preferences and values of citizens.[50]

Secondly, in order to enhance the representative qualities of participants and the accountability of administrators, staffs should seek to involve local and regional officials more thoroughly and systematically in the planning than was the case in the three studies examined, especially LISS.[51] Tucker argues, for example, that urban and regional planners can provide numerous insights into local conditions and local attitudes.[52] If encouraged to think in broad terms, says Tucker, they "usually come a great deal closer to representing the public interest than any one special interest group."[53] Although the staffs, especially in the CRBP Study, did meet at times with local officials, more effort is needed.[54] At a minimum, the inputs of such individuals may balance concrete interests with an abstract claim of public interest.

Thirdly, the three staffs failed to use a potential tool for providing broad-based information about citizen preferences and attitudes—a poll, or survey—again in part because of the cost involved, but planners have seldom used such instruments in conjunction with Level B planning. As the LISS CAC members recognized and as James advocates, polls constitute a possible means for enhancing the representativeness of the citizen opinions solicited in the course of such investigations.[55] In particular, they offer a means of ascertaining the interests and needs of low-income, minority-group, and working-class individuals who usually do not participate in other ways.[56] At a minimum, a more careful consideration of the applicability of this approach to future studies is desirable.

Even with such changes, the possibility that citizen participants can be truly representative of the public at large seems unlikely. It remains necessary for staff members to involve other interested or affected groups conspicuously absent from the planning activities. One LISS staff member reported that he did so by telephoning the leaders of such organizations to sample their opinions, and he obtained a more balanced view on given issues.[57] But again, the fact that the planners must themselves seek such balance demonstrates the weakness of public participation as a means of holding these same individuals accountable.

Modifying the structural aspects of the programs. Structural problems can be dealt with more successfully. Here two options exist. First, citizen participants can be better integrated into the total planning process by having them advise the other non-NERBC planners. At a minimum this means that staffs would facilitate the involvement of citizens in work groups. A second option would be to centralize the planning structure by giving more control to the NERBC staffs. In this instance the present advisory structure and the level of citizen involvement would suffice, for citizens would be interacting with planners clearly in charge of the studies, a position of power the LISS, SENE, and CRBP staff members did not enjoy. This latter option clearly seems the most meaningful of the two and is a strategy that is currently gaining favor at the federal level. NERBC's more recent Lake Champlain (Level B) Study exemplifies this approach.[58]

Improving the timing of participation. Many of the problems of timing can also be lessened. The early delays in involving citizens can be overcome in either of two ways. First, the NERBC chairman could directly appoint all advisory committee members. In view of the political reasons for involving the states in this selection, a more acceptable plan might be to provide that, if the governors did not make the appointments within a period of 45 or, perhaps, 60 days, the NERBC chairman would do so.[59] This second approach seems less likely than the first to result in committees being a mirror image of the river basin commission or its chairman.[60] Later delays might be avoided by selecting alternate members initially or by employing similar deadlines.

To avoid an abrupt end to citizen involvement after plan formulation, an ongoing advisory structure to the Commission itself should be established. The Ohio River Basin Commission (ORBC), for example, created such a central CAC, which in turn helped to organize specific CAC's for its Level B studies.[61] Membership in these two groups overlapped. If used in future NERBC studies, this arrangement would provide for the continued involvement of skilled and informed citizens in the Commission's activities and thus for the ongoing supervision of the NERBC administrators.

Clarifying the participants' roles. Still other activities might serve to alleviate the problems related to the roles played by citizens. In general, though it is appropriate for citizens and staff members to involve a broad range of interests in the public participation programs, both groups should acknowledge that neither advisory committee members nor the citizens who attend public meetings are likely to represent the public at large, and they should define the participants' roles accordingly.[62]

In particular, the formalism enveloping citizen roles in such studies, as reflected in voting and other procedures used by LISS, SENE, and CRBP advisory committees, might usefully be reduced.[63] Generally, the members adopted formal recommendations, directed to respective staffs, which were acceptable to at least a majority of the individual advisers. However, this process frequently involved lengthy debate within the committees, which in the end resulted in statements constituting the lowest common denominator of the opinions expressed. Given the time spent in debating over phrasing and the generality of the statements produced, the value of these collective efforts seems questionable. Less emphasis should be placed on formal recommendations and more on informal, more detailed advice.

Regardless of whether the comments are received formally or informally, planners would be well advised to develop a system for listing citizen recommendations and for reporting their staff's reaction to them.[64] This procedure would help to ensure that citizen comments would be properly examined; also it would bolster the morale of the citizens.

Informing citizens about the studies. Finally, some means may be suggested for better informing citizens so as to increase their knowledge and awareness of the studies. The major need is for a more continuous and aggressive information program than that found in LISS, SENE, and CRBP. Although the LISS Study probably received better newspaper coverage than its two counterparts, mass media coverage in all three occurred largely at the times of the public meetings, leaving gaps during the intervening periods.

More media coverage during these times is essential; that requires in part more rigorous staff efforts to obtain free media coverage.

In LISS the publication of the *Urban Sea* supplemented such media coverage, although it is difficult to assess the impact of this tool on the level of public information about the study. Clearly it had its limits. The *Urban Sea* appeared only four times, usually at the time of public meetings, and reached a relatively small audience. To be effective this type of publication requires broader and more frequent distribution. An alternative to this approach would be for the staff of a given study or its parent commission to issue a newsletter, using an expanded mailing list.[65] Still other approaches might be devised. Hanchey, for example, advocates the use of traveling displays, which might be located at public events likely to be attended by citizens interested in some aspect of water resources. Such displays could be used to distribute further information about studies of this type.[66]

Acceptance of these various suggestions would help to inform more citizens about such studies, about the regional nature of water-related problems, and about the agencies responsible for carrying out planning tasks. It must be acknowledged, however, that piecemeal efforts by small staffs cannot reach and bear the burden of educating the masses of citizens in a region on water resources issues.

In summary, by increasing the breadth of citizen involvement, by restructuring the planning programs, by improving the timing of public participation, by clarifying the roles of the participants, and by better informing citizens about planning problems and activities, bureaucratic accountability could be improved in studies of this type. More meaningful citizen input into the studies would result, and the problems of accountability discussed above would be reduced. In part, these improvements require that an increased percentage of the budget of Level B studies be spent in public participation activities. There is a need to develop a crude target figure (or range) for such expenditures.

It is also evident, however, that even at best such alterations in the public participation programs will not totally overcome these varied problems, and that citizen participation will remain an imperfect means for making administrators answerable to the public at large. Time and monetary constraints are likely to limit efforts to improve the quality of citizen participation. Nevertheless, the record of these studies indicates that, in conjunction with other methods, citizen participation did make important advances in enhancing administrative accountability. It resulted in more effective and responsive plans for water resources utilization than would have been created had the planners been left to their own devices.

CHAPTER SIX

Participation and Accountability

Public participation remains a concept enveloped in controversy. Students of the problem who are skeptical about the merits of participation suggest that the strategies to democratize policy-making by involving citizens do not and cannot work. Some critics offer the fatalistic view that citizens cannot genuinely influence or control administrators; in the process of attempting to do so, they are frequently coopted. Others argue that to the extent that citizens are integrated into the policy-making process, the rationality of the process is degraded by parochialism and emotionalism.

From another perspective, a different set of writers view public participation as the purest form of democracy. It offers solutions to the problems of big government and, more specifically, bureaucratic accountability. These ideas found their most optimistic expression in the Office of Economic Opportunity and the literature related to the War on Poverty. As evidenced above, neither such dismal fatalism nor such unbridled optimism regarding public participation seems warranted. The following analysis rejects both extremes and presents a view of citizen participation tempered with moderate optimism.

What general lessons about the relationship between public participation and bureaucratic accountability can be drawn from the case studies we have presented? Is citizen involvement likely to enhance accountability in other water resources planning efforts, in water resources policy-making, and in administrative policy-making in general? How can the probability of its doing so be increased? These questions form the central theme in this final chapter.

Participation and Accountability in Water Resources Planning

One must proceed with caution from a case study to generalizations. A particular danger is that the circumstances surrounding the three studies performed by NERBC may have been so special as to void their comparative value. Yet when one reads accounts of other studies, this does not appear to be the case with LISS, SENE, or CRBP.

It must not be forgotten that various factors, which inevitably vary from case to case, affect citizen participation in water resources planning. These include the areal scope of the planning effort, as well as the seriousness and the salience of water-related problems in the area.[1] Mogulof observes that factors at the local level, including distinctly human factors, also shape the impact of citizen participation on a given planning process.[2] In terms of such variables, certain characteristics of the three NERBC studies set them apart from many other water-related planning efforts. It is difficult to speak precisely about the differences, to substantiate their existence, or to assess their impact, yet their distinctive characteristics warrant further discussion.

First, the LISS, SENE, and CRBP studies were of broader scope than many water resources planning investigations. They had a regional focus not shared by investigations that center on the problems of a smaller community. This broad geographical setting affected the basic nature of the three studies and of citizen involvement in them. As befits regional (Level B) studies, their recommendations tended to be both general and long term. In addition, the task of integrating the diverse population distributed over the three respective regions into each planning process proved difficult and required a particularly complex and rigorous public participation program.[3] One would expect citizens to be more likely to get involved in and to express sharp differences of opinion over projects of a more immediate (local) and more specific nature, such as a Level C study.[4] That the LISS and SENE plans encompassed a broad range of functional topics also necessitated an especially elaborate public information program.[5]

Secondly, the geographical setting of LISS, SENE, and CRBP affected the salience of the water-related concerns being discussed, the general proclivity of citizens to participate in the programs, and the attention given by participants to local concerns. Water-related issues are less important in New England and adjacent areas than in many regions where water is in critically short supply or where flooding occurs more frequently. Construction-oriented agencies therefore play a diminished role in water resources problem-solving in New England and other areas in the Northeast.[6] Accordingly, the priority of water-related issues remains low in the region, a condition that tended to lessen participation in the studies.[7] Citizens who participated in the New England studies brought a less constructionist approach to water resources planning than do their counterparts in other regions. The literature suggests, however, that citizen involvement in governmental activities has traditionally been more pronounced and more organized in New England than in many other regions, and this fact served to compensate in terms of participation for the low salience of the issues and to bring the planners in contact with well established groups.[8] Furthermore, the role of local (as distinct from county) government is more pronounced in New England than in the South and many other areas.[9] This made it particularly difficult to interest citizens in a regional project and to get them to consider solutions involving government beyond the boundaries of their own communities.

Thirdly, the New England River Basins Commission is a unique organization. It lacks the constructionist attitude that authors frequently attribute to the more traditional water resources agencies.[10] In the course of the studies, NERBC also embraced the concept of citizen participation more fully than have many other such organizations. Perhaps, this reflected the fact that it was created only a decade ago, as well as the absence of supportive clientele groups. Undoubtedly, NERBC's openness has contributed to its generally good public image and to the support it has earned from civic groups like the League of Women Voters. In any case, one must suspect that public participation achieved what it did in these studies at least partially because the Commission's leadership displayed a genuine desire to work cooperatively with citizens. In generalizing about LISS, SENE, and CRBP, one must keep in mind, then, the regional focus of Level B investigations, their New England setting, and the unique aspects of NERBC itself.

Certain of these factors worked to increase the number of individuals participating; others had the opposite effect. Thus it is difficult to predict what might happen elsewhere. Given the tradition of participation in New England and surrounding areas, many other regions may find it difficult to involve citizens within a regional setting to a comparable extent. A higher level of citizen involvement may well be possible, however, in locally oriented water resources studies there or elsewhere. It also seems likely that citizen participation in regions which are expanding or which lack adequate water supplies may involve both a less conservationist orientation and more sharp conflicts of opinions than found in LISS, SENE, and CRBP. Participation in areas outside New England and Long Island may evoke less concern for the prerogatives of local governments and less involvement by organized interest groups. Differences between these three studies and other water-related planning efforts exist, then, but are of degree rather than kind and do not prohibit generalizing from the findings providing reasonable caution is taken.

An examination of citizen involvement in LISS, SENE, and CRBP provides numerous insights into the effects of public participation on bureaucratic accountability in water resources planning and policy-making. The problems identified and the impacts documented above are likely to be replicated in other such planning and policy-making efforts. Similarly, the suggestions for improvement offered in the previous chapter also apply to other such planning studies. When further differences are considered (see below), these case studies provide insights into the effects of public participation on the accountability of bureaucrats working in other substantive policy areas.

Effects of participation on the accountability of water resources planners. The precise impact of public participation on bureaucratic accountability varies somewhat from one water resources planning effort to another, depending upon numerous variables. Yet at best, citizen participation serves as a limited and imperfect mechanism for sustaining accountable water resources bureaucracies. It is limited in effectiveness in the sense that the citizens are advisers only and lack significant authority over the personnel in charge of planning investigations. Moreover, in water resources planning efforts generally, as in the three NERBC studies, several additional factors limit the suitability of citizen participation as a mechanism for holding planners accountable. These problems reflect some of the concerns voiced by authors critical of public participation, namely that such involvement is unrepresentative and parochial. Other problems have also surfaced in the course of my research.

The above case studies support the generally accepted notion that citizen participants in water resources planning tend to be unrepresentative of the general public. Unless faced with serious water-related problems, most citizens are not likely to become interested in, informed about, or involved in water resources planning. These tendencies reflect ingrained public attitudes and cannot easily be changed. Greater turnout at meetings or the establishment of more formal channels for selecting citizen representatives—while desirable—will not alter this basic situation. An additional imperfection here is that the burden of ensuring a broad sampling of public opinion has come to rest primarily with the administrators themselves, the very people regulated by the mechanisms of participation. Moreover, individuals who do participate frequently voice local, self-interested concerns, at times at the expense of regional or other more general issues. The literature of political culture suggests that these orientations to politics are in part culturally rooted and of apparently long duration.[11]

The above case studies also reveal various structural impediments, such as the elaborate division of responsibilities within investigations, which limit citizen participation in water resources planning. Because of the number of agencies involved in many planning projects and the way in which currently they are only loosely coordinated, these impediments are widespread. Significantly, even apart from their adverse effect on participation, the characteristics of water resources planning diminish administrative accountability by making it difficult to fix responsibility for planning decisions and other activities. Barring a reorganization of the agencies or a fundamental change in the way in which they are coordinated, these impediments will continue to limit the ability of citizens to make themselves heard.

Problems of timing and role definition arise repeatedly whenever citizens are integrated into a planning effort. They may be dealt with more successfully than the above difficulties, but they are not readily surmounted. With regard to timing, the use of complex selection formulae for advisers—with their attendant problems—seems likely to continue because of the various levels of government interested in water-related matters, even where relatively small amounts of territory are involved.[12] Moreover, Hanchey has observed that public interest in planning studies typically is low at their start and matures over time.[13] Thus it is and will continue to be difficult to get citizens involved early in a project, even beyond the inherent difficulties associated with the initial selection process. Citizen influence over planners will therefore be limited during this crucial period of formulation. Similarly, problems of role definition are likely to be recurrent, although more substantial guidelines from the Water Resources Council could alleviate this problem.

Related to these, but less evident in the case studies than in other water-related planning efforts, is the added complication that citizens, starting with different concerns, may be unable to agree on solutions to particular problems or on the nature of the problems themselves. Frequently, water-related problems are not self-evident, nor is agreement simply the product of better information or communication.[14] Where consensus among citizens is absent, the ability of participation mechanisms like public hearings to resolve conflicts involving water resources issues seems limited. Such conflicts reduce both the influence of citizen participants in the making of certain crucial planning decisions and their ability to supervise administrators.[15]

In summary, this study gives additional substance to many of the general comments in the literature about the shortcomings of citizen participation as a mechanism for providing accountability in water resources planning or other administrative activities. Certain of these criticisms about the unrepresentative and parochial nature of citizen involvement appear well grounded, although other concerns—such as that participation would hamper planning efficiency—find little support here. Other problems related to the planning structures, timing, and role definition also limit the potential of public participation as a mechanism for holding water resources planners answerable to the public at large.

Despite these problems, citizen involvement does, in various ways, enhance administrative accountability in water resources planning. The findings of the case studies reinforce many of the positive arguments raised by proponents of the concept. These appear readily applicable to water resources planning as a whole and serve to overcome some of the problems that have been identified above.

As Berger observes, there appears to be in every region: "a reservoir of citizens concerned about their water resources, informed on major planning issues, and willing to work hard on plan formulation if given a proper opportunity to do so." [16] This group includes individuals with environmental interests, as were found in the NERBC studies, but may also include those with interests of a different nature, perhaps more business or property oriented. In general, participation programs offer individuals and groups who lack various political resources but are interested in water-related questions an opportunity to express their opinions directly to governmental decision-makers and to have at least a limited voice in the planning process. Public meetings prove particularly helpful in this regard, provided that they are well publicized.

Problems of representativeness and parochialism notwithstanding, the citizens who participate bring to water resources planning investigations a particular knowledge of local conditions and a range of interests and values, which, while limited, is likely to exceed that of the planners. Probably the most notable accomplishment to date of such participants in the three case studies and other water-related investigations has been the airing of environmental and social concerns. As assessments of water resources planning by the National Water Commission and other observers have shown and as one recent court decision involving off-shore oil drilling has demonstrated, environmental issues have frequently been ignored by water resources planners.[17] Citizen participation helps to correct this imbalance. The same is true of social concerns. In part because of citizen pressure, water-related plans must take into consideration the objective of "social well-being."[18] Citizens continue to serve as watchdogs over such issues.

As exemplified in the NERBC studies, citizen participation also aids in alleviating other widely recognized deficiencies in planning, including the tendencies to (1) adhere rigidly to long-range forecasts; (2) overemphasize the use of benefit-cost calculations; (3) avoid setting priorities; and (4) ignore related land-use implications.[19] Citizen inputs, then, result in more responsible water resources plans, which are both more effective and responsive— more in accord with public needs and preferences—than would otherwise be the case.

Bureaucratic accountability is also enhanced in water resources planning by the extent to which citizen participation under this advisory rubric fosters other channels of control over administrators. Because the citizens function as advisers, they do not automatically detract from or impede alternate means of providing for accountability. Instead these public-participation programs supply those who choose to become regularly involved with considerable information about planning issues and activities in this policy area. To that extent they help to create more informed citizens. Citizens may use this newly acquired knowledge to generate reviews of administrative undertakings by other political institutions.

For example, as seen in the three studies, complaints from informed citizens to their congressmen or state legislators invited greater legislative scrutiny of the resources planning efforts. Such a response is particularly likely to be forthcoming when the complainants are themselves officially associated with the studies. Although it did not occur in these cases, citizens may also use their knowledge about the planning of studies to pursue legal action through the courts, thereby increasing the control of legal institutions over water-oriented bureaucracies. Checks of this type have become increasingly important in recent years, especially since the passage of NEPA. With this recourse in mind, Sax observes that, at a minimum, what citizen involvement in planning might achieve is to inform people and to prepare them for future action.[20]

Should citizens address their comments to other executive officials, for example, in either the Water Resources Council or the White House, accountability through this channel would be increased. In addition, as professionals with areas of expertise related to water resources serve as science or citizen advisers, accountability to fellow professionals is augmented. Finally, as seen above, citizen comments directed at agencies responsible for loosely coordinating planning efforts may also help to increase their control over the planning efforts, thus streamlining the lines of accountability in such studies.

To summarize, citizen participation is not a panacea for the problems of bureaucratic accountability in water resources planning. Even under present arrangements, final planning decisions are made by administrators who enjoy considerable discretionary powers. They, too, are responsible for orchestrating involvement in the studies of the very individuals who seek to influence and supervise them. Numerous imperfections mar the citizen participation strategy. Moreover, it does not in itself deal with certain basic characteristics of water resources planning, such as the large number of agencies involved and the difficulties inherent in fixing responsibility, which both impede participation and cause additional problems of accountability. Yet despite all these limitations, public participation serves to enhance rather than diminish bureaucratic accountability—by resulting in more responsive and effective plans and by complementing various other means of controlling administrators, via the Congress, the courts, the President, or fellow professionals. Citizen participation is a significant but by no means complete or radical reform.

Having acknowledged these benefits, as well as the accompanying problems, it seems desirable to say that citizen participants should be limited to an advisory role in water resources planning. Because the *problem* of representativeness seems inherent in public participation in water resources planning, citizen participants should not be granted actual decision-making authority in planning decisions. Such an act would create tensions between this strategy and other modes of providing accountability, would make lines of accountability in an already diffuse decision-making structure all the more obscure, and would, perhaps, make water resources planning even more elitist than it is at present.

Enhancing the accountability of water resources planners. Within such an advisory framework, however, various steps are needed in order to increase the utility of citizen participation. Here again the comments made above with regard to the case studies seem applicable. The representativeness of the participants needs to be improved by expanding both the numbers of citizens participating (especially minority-group members) and the breadth of their focus; by involving more local officials, including planners; and by using surveys were applicable. There is also a need to integrate citizen advisers into the working sessions of the planning process. Where many agencies are involved, the citizens should be attached to one organization clearly in charge of the planning effort. In terms of timing, participation should be more continuous throughout the planning process, beginning early and extending into the implementation period. The role of the participants ought to be better and more uniformly defined. Citizen comments should be handled and responded to systematically. Finally, more aggressive public participation programs, which in part use advisory group members to foster two-way communication between planners and affected interests, are needed.

In general one is struck by the largely experimental nature of citizen participation. The guidance given to water resources planners by federal laws and administrative standards is minimal.[21] This is reflected in the Water Resources Council's "Principles and Standards." Planning staffs lack a clear understanding of the goals and objectives to be pursued in involving citizens in the planning process.[22] As a result, participation programs have been established in a random rather than systematic manner. Staffs have exchanged little information about the structure of such programs; little conventional wisdom exists as to how participation can be improved.

Given this state of the art, several specific needs may be identified. The first is the need to develop more systematic standards.[23] Guidelines should be established concerning the funding of expenses incurred by advisory committees. As Mogulof comments, federal policy in this area has been erratic.[24] Secondly, further evaluations should be undertaken to determine what participation has in practice achieved and what strategies have worked best, so that programs can be restructured accordingly.[25] Thirdly, there exists a need for more training programs for planners, such as the seminars initiated by the Environmental Protection Agency for "208" planners.[26] Currently, then, citizen participation has in a limited fashion enhanced bureaucratic accountability and responsible water planning. Further changes will permit it to do an even better job in this regard, within an advisory framework.

It is also clear, however, that there are problems of accountability in water resources planning which citizen participation cannot resolve. Other reforms, such as reorganization and centralization, are necessary. In the end, what citizen participation achieves in any given study is likely to be less than ideal and will depend upon how the individual planners use the information provided.[27] In short, citizen participation can encourage the development of responsible water plans; it cannot create them.

Accountability of Officials in the Water Policy Subsystem

Those who undertake water-related planning investigations are a vital part of the policy-making process. Their plans serve as the basis for other policy-making activities; the quality of the plans has a significant impact on the caliber of later policy decisions. It is also important, however, to assess the effects of citizen involvement on the accountability of the other policy-makers, including high-level administrators, who are removed from the initial planning process and who are responsible for translating the completed plans into authorized, funded, and implemented federal projects. In general, what impact does citizen participation have on the authorization, funding, and implementation of responsible water resources policies?

As Fritschler observes, there exist in different policy areas, political subsystems comprised of the individuals and groups who make or influence governmental decisions related to those concerns.[28] In the realm of water resources, the primary actors in the policy subsystem are the leaders of several Congressional committees and subcommittees, individual congressmen from potentially affected areas, certain officials of water-related agencies, representatives of various clientele groups, and the members of the National Rivers and Harbors Congress, which includes many of the above.[29] Collectively, they dominate the authorization and appropriation processes by which water projects are established.

Water resources policy, typical of public policy-making, has long been made "in a spirit of friendly and quiet cooperation between small segments of Congress, the bureaucracy, and the interest group community."[30] Environmental groups, the Office of Management and Budget, and, most recently, President Carter—in his attempt to stop the funding of some thirty water projects—have sought to end the exclusivity of this policy-making arrangement. The results of their challenge are mixed, at best. Carter's efforts in 1977 encountered vigorous opposition in Congress, and funding for more than a majority of the projects was eventually approved.

For many observers, the way in which water-related decisions are made and the resultant policies exemplify much of what is wrong with American public policy-making. Several blue ribbon panels—for example, the Second Hoover Commission's Task Force on Water Resources and Power—have called for changes in both the structure for making water policies and in the policies themselves, policy and process being inextricably linked.[31] More specifically, criticisms of the process have centered on the perceived lack of both objectivity and concern for the public interest. The initiative for policies, the critics charge, typically comes from agencies with vested interests in completing the projects.

Moreover, Congressional involvement in water policy-making focuses on individual representatives or senators who are interested in securing projects for their constituencies, rather than on Congress as a collective body. This reflects the shared attitude among the members, in part based on concern for reelection, that a congressman should represent the interests of the voters who elected him or her to office. Thus mutual accommodation prevails.[32] A congressman usually does not intervene in the decision-making process unless it concerns a project in his or her district.[33] Congress' reliance on committees, its seniority system (despite some relaxation of these rules), and the specialization prevalent among its members reinforce these tendencies.[34] Generally, this situation allows the lobbyists for client groups to concentrate their forces on key members, the resultant policies being shaped by the logic of pork barrel politics.[35]

This process, say the critics, leads to the adoption of policies of questionable rationality. According to Helen Ingram and others, water policies in the United States are too project oriented; there are no broad discussions of goals and alternatives—a situation that leads to inconsistent and often contradictory policies.[36] Moreover, these policies do not respond to "economic and physical facts" or "social and environmental forces."[37] Too few individuals or groups benefit. The problems carry over to the implementation stage, which is dominated by these same interests.

Needless to say, many individuals, particularly the principals involved, dispute this assessment of water resources policy-making; for me, however, the above provides an accurate assessment of the current situation. The question, then, becomes: "Does (or can) citizen participation enhance the accountability of the high-level administrators and congressmen who are part of the water resources subsystem?" Can participation increase the likelihood that more responsible water-related policies will result?

That is a difficult question. At present some citizens participate in the process by which water policies are formally enacted (authorized and funded), but their level and means of involvement vary considerably. It is even harder to track and assess the amount of influence they have than was the case with the planning studies examined above.

Citizen involvement at these later stages of decision-making does not consist primarily of public participation in administrative activities, in the sense that I have used the term. There is little direct contact between the policy-making leadership of the various water-related agencies and interested citizens. Instead, citizens become involved in policy-making through the more traditional means of participation: (1) contacting individual congressmen; (2) testifying at formal hearings; (3) serving on special commissions or task forces; and (4) being members of permanent advisory bodies, like the Citizens' Advisory Committee on Environmental Quality. These latter two bodies differ, however, from committees like the LISS CAC, in that they are not so likely to become immersed in either the operations of given water-related agencies or the substance of particular projects. Finally, citizens also participate during the implementation stage of projects by filing suits to stop them, or in some other way affect them.[38]

In general, direct participation by citizens during the authorization and funding stages of water resources policy-making is much less systematic than at the earlier planning stages; nor are the requirements for participation as specific. Unless a particular task force should choose to hold hearings outside of Washington and in the affected region or regions, participation will normally occur on a relatively small scale, involving few citizens from the areas in question. All of these conditions exacerbate the problems of representativeness, timing, and lack of information, discussed above. Moreover, these contacts are likely to be formal, in contrast to the frequently informal relationships between citizens and planners. Because of such characteristics, the influence of the citizenry over the relevant administrators and congressmen during these later policy-making stages does not appear to be significant.

More specific limitations on the influence of citizens who testify at hearings or belong to advisory bodies can also be identified. First, while certain citizens speaking at public hearings come in part from public interest groups and environmental organizations, the political resources and the influence of such group representatives or of other unaffiliated individuals seldom match those of client groups. Secondly, citizens who serve on ad hoc commissions have very limited influence over the officials creating project-oriented water policies. Panels, during their temporary existence, focus on broad issues rather than the merits of individual projects; yet these projects form the bulk of water-related legislation. Thirdly, the influence of permanent advisory bodies is circumscribed, that of the Citizens' Advisory Committee on Environmental Quality providing a case in point. The Committee met only three times in 1975 and, according to its annual report for that year, did not address issues related to domestic water usage.[39] Thus during this period the impact of this major advisory committee on the issues raised above was minimal. These problems retard the efforts of direct participation.

Furthermore, citizens continue to participate indirectly in authorization and funding decisions. They do so through the written summaries of public reactions to respective plans which many planning agencies submit to the Water Resources Council, the President, and, eventually, the Congress as part of, or along with, their final planning documents. For example, the LISS, SENE, and CRBP plans each contained a section summarizing the major comments about the plan received from both public agencies and citizens.[40] A knowledge of citizen recommendations permits individual congressmen to better represent the interests of their local constituents during these later policy-making stages. Yet although such citizen inputs *seem* important, it is impossible within the limits of this investigation to assess the impact they have had on the bureaucrats and congressmen (or legislative aides) who read them. The assumption is that they have at least read them.

What is clear is that several problems beset the use of these summaries, as reflected in Warner's call for a "reviewable record" of public participation.[41] Not all planning agencies produce such documentation, and no satisfactory standards have been established for what should be included in the summaries. For example, the three NERBC staffs made commendable efforts to summarize and respond directly to citizen recommendations, using an outline format. However, their summaries could have been improved by separating the comments of the citizens from those of the reviewing agencies and by providing a more substantive discussion of the citizens' comments and the staffs' reactions to them. One danger is that summaries may not supply later reviewers with enough information about citizens' views to make the information usable.

Such reviewable records of public involvement in these planning stages may permit citizens to influence indirectly subsequent decisions about the plans. Whether this occurs depends on the quality of the initial comments, the receptivity of the reviewers to the ideas expressed, and the basic adequacy of the written record provided. Further efforts are necessary, to ensure that the last condition is met.

Thus by both direct and indirect means citizens do at present participate in the formal enactment of water resources policies. The nature and the extent of this involvement, however, differs significantly from public participation in the earlier planning processes of given projects. In short, the participation phenomenon has not permeated the authorization and funding stages of policy-making to the extent that it has the initial planning ones. It may be in part responsible for some changes in current project-oriented water policies, such as greater concern for environmental and social costs. Nevertheless, to date, genuine public involvement in the later stages of public policy-making has been very limited and has not alleviated the basic deficiencies associated with the authorization and funding processes.

This is also true of the impact of citizen participation during the implementation stage of policy-making. Citizen involvement at this point, often through the use of the courts, has been a sporadic process marked by uneven results. In some instances citizen suits have blocked what might reasonably be called projects of dubious value; yet the courts have tended both to defer to administrative expertise and to resolve cases along procedural lines.[42] All have limited citizen influence, as have the various technical restraints on judicial power, including the concepts of standing and *stare decisis*.[43]

Still other individuals become involved in the implementation stages of policy-making by staying in contact with either the agency performing the task or congressmen with an interest in it. Although few authors have systematically studied the accomplishments of citizens who participate during the implementation process, it seems reasonable to suppose that their involvement is also characterized by sporadic and uneven results.

Thus, citizen involvement in the authorization, funding, and implementation stages of policy-making has not, to date, significantly enhanced the accountability of the governmental members of the water policy subsystem or the quality of water resources policies. In this respect, the current beneficial effects of public participation in these later stages of policy-making, where it is more infrequent in timing and uneven in results, are not commensurate with those of citizen involvement in the earlier planning processes.

Increasing the opportunities for citizen participation offers one potential means for enhancing the accountability of the administrative and congressional officials who control the authorization, funding, and implementation of water-related policies. Probably the most serious problem is the narrowness of the concerns that presently enter into and dominate these stages of the process. Current policies are geared to the needs of certain agencies (organizational survival), constituent groups (money and jobs for the district), and particular clients (services at little cost). Just as it does in the earlier planning processes, citizen participation provides a way of introducing a new and somewhat broader set of concerns, including long-neglected environmental and social ones, into these calculations. To fulfill this promise, however, the role of citizens during these later stages of policy-making must be enlarged. Given considerable public apathy, the centering of most high-level decision-making activities in Washington—together with the closed, complex nature of the policy-making process—this cannot be readily achieved.

Citizen participation in these later stages can and should be increased. Some expense, some inconvenience, and some dangers (since the citizens are not truly representative) will result, but not in any extreme degree.[44] The more serious obstacle is that public participation in these stages of policy-making seems likely to be highly limited, even at best, although it can be increased in several ways: (1) fostering contacts between citizens and congressmen, such as by holding more public meetings outside of the nation's capital; (2) providing more information to citizens about water policies and priorities; and (3) improving the documentation of citizen responses to earlier planning documents. The last would require the creation of a more complete record of public comments than is now typically produced; more uniform guidelines for such summaries are needed. One possibility is that citizen advisers might themselves produce a record. The citizens involved in LISS, SENE, and CRBP made no detailed, collective effort near the end of their respective studies; but then, they were not asked to do so. The 1971 report by the Citizens Review Committee on the Connecticut River Comprehensive Study shows, given certain conditions, what is possible in this regard.[45] In general, such reforms would increase citizen influence in these later policy-making stages both by involving them more directly and by attaching greater meaning and importance to their earlier inputs. It is probably not desirable to create more advisory panels at these higher levels, however, because of the problems of representativeness associated with such groups.[46]

It also seems logical that as citizens participate more systematically in planning investigations, they will develop more interest in local and regional water resources programs. This heightened interest may spur their involvement in the subsequent authorization, funding, and implementation stages, making them more inclined to make contact with administrators and legislators about their concerns. Even with these developments, however, it is difficult to imagine increased participation overcoming many of these problems. It is more difficult to involve citizens here than it is in the earlier planning stages.

Significant improvement in this part of the policy-making process and in the final policies themselves requires primarily an improvement in our traditional political institutions. That might be usefully pursued through a number of different ways, including (1) Congressional and election reform; (2) establishment of a public advocacy agency; (3) a comprehensive, long-term approach to water policy-making; (4) emphasis upon environmental and social concerns in the training of water resources planners and engineers; (5) reorganization and consolidation of the water-related executive agencies; and (6) more substantive involvement by the courts. In pursuing such reforms, care must be taken not to circumscribe unduly the powers of administrative decision-makers.

To summarize, citizen participation, despite its many limitations, offers a significant way of enhancing the accountability of water resources planners and of improving the quality of water-related plans. It has brought forth additional information and additional perspectives for planners to consider and should therefore be encouraged. Citizen involvement in the later authorization, appropriation, and implementation stages of policy-making has not, however, kept pace with those developments. Further studies about public participation in these stages are needed; it seems clear that it is now highly restricted. These later stages are dominated by senior administrators, key legislators, and others who comprise the water policy subsystem. All too often these individuals fail to create policies that serve the interests of the public at large. As seen, many more specific problems can be identified.

Citizens play both direct and indirect roles in these later policy-making decisions, but highly limited ones. For example, their specific comments about given plans, made during the initial planning investigations, have less impact in these subsequent stages than is warranted. Ensuring that an adequate reviewable record of such citizen inputs exists is one way of increasing citizen influence. Still other reforms, aimed at facilitating citizen involvement, are required. In the end, however, public participation in authorization, funding, and implementation decisions is unlikely to enhance significantly the accountability of the administrators and key legislators who comprise the water policy-making subsystem or to increase the quality of the final water resources policies. Other types of political reforms, such as reorganization, are needed first.

Conclusions

The above case studies and discussions of citizen participation in water resources planning and decision-making encourage one to reflect at a more general level on bureaucratic power in public policy-making and the role that citizens can play in enhancing administrative accountability and responsible public policy. Certain cautions must be observed, for the roles played by administrators and citizen advisers vary from one policy area to another. For example, the problems of administrative accountability seem especially severe in the realm of water resources because of (1) the power of the major agencies, (2) the low salience in some areas of the issues involved, (3) the highly fragmented nature of the decision-making structure, and (4) the technical nature of much of the enterprise. All of this suggests that water resources administrators enjoy greater autonomy than many of their counterparts in other policy areas. With regard to the role of citizens, similar differences occur. Citizen involvement appears more feasible in more compact,

shorter-term, more locally oriented programs, such as those dealing with community development. In contrast, it seems far less
practicable in the areas of foreign affairs and defense, where the
need for secrecy has long been recognized by most observers, despite their disagreement over how much secrecy is desirable.[47]

Nevertheless, the above findings are broadly applicable to most
policy areas. The particular successes and failures of public participation have been, or may be, replicated in other fields. For example, citizen involvement in former War on Poverty programs
and current Community Development programs has similarly suf-
fered from problems of representativeness, role-definition, program structure, timing, lack of information, and parochialism.[48]
The above examination, then, provides an appropriate basis for
further discussion.

The NERBC case studies demonstrate the prominent, some-
times predominant, role that bureaucrats play in water resources
planning and policy-making. Administrators are primarily responsible for determining what problems are studied and for conducting the planning investigations that are the foundation upon
which water policies are built. Senior administrators are themselves important members of the political subsystem that controls
the authorization and funding of water projects. Bureaucrats also
dominate the implementation stage of policy-making. In general,
these findings parallel the conclusions of most writers who have
studied administrative involvement in policy formulation in other
issue areas. Clearly, bureaucrats play a major role in public policy-
making, regardless of the substantive area.

Given the many pressures upon administrators to serve essentially private interests, this situation appropriately raises concerns
among many observers. As Woll argues, the growth of bureaucratic powers has fundamentally altered the American constitu-
tional system by causing a breakdown in the primary mechanism—elections—which has traditionally limited the arbitrary
power of government.[49] New or restored mechanisms are needed
to enhance administrative accountability and provide responsible
public policies that are responsive, effective, and lawful.

In designing such mechanisms, however, one must consider the
very indispensability of bureaucracy:

Given the needs of modern government for economic regulation, special-ization, continuity, and speed in the dispatch of business, to mention only a few, it is the bureaucracy that has stepped in to fill the gap created by the inability of other branches to fulfill all of these requirements.[50]

These developments have taken place concurrently in water re-sources and other policy areas. In their pursuit of accountability and in their desires to limit bureaucratic discretion, critics must be careful not to destroy the vitality of these administrative organiza-tions and with it that of American government itself. To be suc-cessful, proposed reforms must balance those two different sets of concerns. As demonstrated above, current efforts at increasing public participation in administrative decision-making offer one reasonable way of addressing the needs.

Within very real limits, the involvement of citizens in admin-istrative policy-making activities in an advisory capacity increases bureaucratic accountability and the formulation of responsible public policies. Public participation is, however, not a flawless mechanism. Because of low turnout, the citizens who participate are usually not genuinely representative of the public at large. Low-income, minority-group, and working-class individuals are often not adequately involved. Problems of role-definition, pro-gram structure, and limited information recur. The parochial interests of citizens may run contrary to the expertise of the ad-ministrators.[51] The timing of citizen involvement usually proves suboptimal. In addition, there exist the ever-present dangers that an influential group of citizens, in their quest for public services, may coopt an agency into serving narrow interests or that an agency, in its quest for survival or aggrandizement, may manipu-late a group of citizens. Frauenglass maintains that a citizen ad-visory board is "often placed between the public and the agency and then used to promote management plans and proposals and to discharge public animosity toward the agency."[52] The above case studies show, however, that advisory groups are capable of serving more honorable purposes. In general these various problems de-tract from but do not destroy the value of citizen participation as a means of enhancing accountability. In practice no mechanisms for providing accountability function ideally; citizen participation is not atypical. In most aspects of government there is a "basic gap between political theory and political process."[53]

Despite its limitations, public participation serves in many ways to increase administrative accountability and the likelihood that public policies will be responsible. Citizens contributed to the NERBC studies by (1) supplying pertinent information about local conditions; (2) evaluating the methodological approaches, priorities, and assumptions of the planners; (3) raising broad, but related value questions; (4) calling the planners' attention to immediate problems; and (5) making the plans more politically acceptable. These inputs helped to increase the accountability of the administrators involved and to make the final LISS, SENE, and CRBP plans more responsive and effective. Other interested citizens have had, or can have, comparable impacts on planning or other administrative policy-making activities in water resources and other substantive areas. Moreover, the involvement of citizen advisers in administrative policy-making activities complements other mechanisms for accountability.

Public policy-making, in its many stages, is an exclusive process. Virtually every policy area is dominated by a political subsystem with a limited membership, including bureaucratic actors. Unavoidably, the policies that result are limited by the perspectives, desires, and experiences of the administrators and other subsystem members. Citizen participation, while not truly representative, expands this process significantly by encouraging examination of additional important concerns that would not otherwise be considered. In the area of water resources, citizen participants have influenced planners and other policy-makers to pay greater attention to long-ignored environmental and social concerns. Similarly, citizens involved in various urban programs have urged planners and other policy-makers to take into account social concerns and the needs of minority groups.

In short, citizen participation provides an additional voice or group of voices to a closed policy-making process. Thus, despite its many limitations, it increases the likelihood that administrative policy-makers will be motivated to serve the public at large and that responsible public policies will result. This would be even more the case if a broader range of people would participate, particularly during the later stages of policy-making. It is difficult to distinguish between the needs of clients or constituents and those of the public at large.[54] Yet the distinction exists and must be recognized; citizen participation aids in ensuring that the latter's needs are considered.

Because of the varied problems associated with public participation, citizen involvement in administrative policy-making should be limited to an advisory role. The alternative, granting decision-making authority to citizens, would only replace other imperfect means of providing accountability with an equally flawed mechanism. An advisory, hence complementary, role is more appropriate.

Within this framework some improvements in policy have been realized, although there is considerable room for improvement. Citizen participation is an uneven process within and among different policy areas. Some flexibility in the structure of public participation programs is appropriate to accommodate the demands of different fields; yet the current lack of uniform standards is unjustified. At present, as Doerksen and Pierce note, the situation "is one of change, jockeying for position, uncertainty, and conflict."[55] Overall, citizens have not been sufficiently integrated into the policy-making process, especially at the crucial authorization and funding stages.

A number of suggestions for improving this situation and thereby enhancing bureaucratic accountability and the quality of public policies have been offered above. These include (1) expanding current public participation and public information programs; (2) setting more uniform standards for citizen involvement; (3) better defining the roles of citizen participants; (4) carefully and concisely documenting citizen comments; (5) training administrators to work cooperatively with citizens; and (6) establishing procedures to evaluate public participation strategies and techniques. A significant effort is needed to involve citizens in public policy-making in a more meaningful way.

I have also shown, however, that there are various problems of administrative accountability—in water resources and in other policy areas—which citizen participation is incapable of rectifying. It cannot, for example, overcome the problems associated with a highly fragmented decision-making structure. For this reason it seems appropriate to think of public participation as one of several interrelated means by which bureaucratic accountability and responsible public policy can be realized. It is generally compatible with the efforts to strengthen the accountability of administrators to the Congress, the President, the courts, and fellow professionals. Public participation should therefore be pursued along with, rather than instead of, these other means for providing bureaucratic accountability.

Research Methodology

In this examination of citizen participation in three major planning efforts undertaken by the New England River Basins Commission, the Long Island Sound Study, the Southeastern New England Study, and the Connecticut River Basin Program, a varied approach has been taken. It has included the following:

1. Examination of public participation materials and other publications of NERBC and its three studies. In particular, I have focused on the draft and final plans of the three studies and the degree to which they reflect public comments. The respective staffs proved extremely cooperative in furnishing copies of all materials requested.
2. Observation of numerous advisory group meetings and public meetings over a two-year period, as well as a review of minutes of meetings that took place before the research began.
3. Interviews with NERBC staff members, members of the advisory groups associated with the studies, and other individuals involved in the projects. Even more important is the time spent conversing with these individuals informally at the many advisory and public meetings.
4. Administration of a survey to citizens attending the final series of public meetings, to examine their background characteristics, their sources of information about the study, the degree of their involvement in the planning process, their evaluation of the public meetings, and their attitudes toward the draft plans produced by the three studies.

The questionnaire was designed and administered by a research team of which I was a member. This team, with administrative headquarters at the Institute for Man and Environment of the University of Massachusetts, was funded by a grant from the U.S. Department of the Interior, Office of Water Research and Technology, to Madge O. Ertel, the Principal Investigator. The questionnaire sought both demographic and attitudinal information from the citizens attending the final series of evening public hearings sponsored by LISS (January 1975), SENE (May and June 1975), and CRBP (February and March 1976). They were held during the official 90-day review period for each study. A few additional items were added to the questionnaire following the LISS meetings.

Those who returned the questionnaire, completed it just before, during, or after that night's meeting. In the course of this survey, the members of the research team personally handed the questionnaires to the people attending, as they registered at the meeting entrance. Prearranged comments by the respective study managers at the beginning of each meeting, the remarks made by the research team members at the time of distribution, and the instructions on the questionnaire itself all directed citizens in attendance to complete the questionnaire and to return it to a research team member when leaving the auditorium.

The design for administering the survey was experimental and contrasted with the use in similar studies of mailed questionnaires and responses. Dissatisfied with the typical return rates of these surveys, I and the other researchers sought to achieve a higher rate of response by conducting the survey at the meetings, thereby broadening the data base of the study and including among the respondents people who would be unlikely to reply to a mailed questionnaire. By design, this process involved an informational trade-off. The process called for a questionnaire shorter than those frequently used in mailed surveys, so as to allow ample opportunity for completion and not to detract from the presentations made at the meetings, yet one which could be expected to produce data more representative and more accurate than that compiled from mailed surveys. A sample of this questionnaire is included in Appendix B.

The number of respondents supports the assumption that this procedure will produce a high rate of response: 1118 people out of a combined audience of about 1400 attendees returned the questionnaire, a response rate of 80 percent. One person in five did not return a questionnaire, despite our efforts. This figure bears examination, even though the explanations offered are impressionistic. Included in this number are most newsmen, many of whom told the researchers that they felt it inappropriate to answer the questionnaire. Confusion about the questionnaire or the process, the constraints of time, and even the use of the questionnaire for note-taking during the meeting account for other nonreturns. One may also speculate that some people identified the survey with the NERBC studies themselves or with their own previous survey efforts, and because of dissatisfaction with the plans or because they had filled out a questionnaire in the past, they chose not to respond. It appears also that some people resist surveys because, among other reasons, they resent the intrusion or fail to see merit in them. There is no firm evidence to suggest, however, that any particular groups of people have been excluded from the data base.

Public Meeting Questionnaire

Southeastern New England Study

This questionnaire is part of a study being conducted by a research team from the University of Massachusetts. The purpose of the project is to evaluate the effectiveness of the Southeastern New England Study's public participation program. Your answers to these brief questions will be very helpful. All individual responses will be kept strictly confidential. You need not sign the questionnaire, but feel free to add any additional comments if you wish.

Please complete the questionnaire while you are at this meeting and return it to a member of the research team as you leave. Your cooperation is greatly appreciated.

1. How did you hear about tonight's public meeting (Check as many as apply)?

    _____ I read about it in the newspaper

    _____ I heard about it on radio or T.V.

    _____ I received a copy of the newspaper "How to Guide Growth in Southeastern New England" in the mail

    _____ Someone told me about the meeting

    _____ I saw someone else's copy of "How to Guide Growth in Southeastern New England."

2. How many other public meetings or hearings on *any* public issues have you attended in the last year?

    _____ 0   _____ 1–5   _____ 5 or more

3. Before you heard about this meeting, did you already know something about the SENE Study?

    _____ Yes   _____ No

If so, how did you hear about the Study in the past?

____ I attended a past public meeting held by the SENE Study

____ I attended a meeting sponsored by another group where I heard about the Study

____ I received a letter from the SENE staff

____ I read about the Study in the newspaper

____ I heard about the Study on radio or T.V.

4. Which of the statements below describe your reasons for coming to this meeting? Please rank them according to their importance to *you* (Most important = 1, Second Most Important = 2, etc. Leave blank those which do not apply.)

____ I am a member of a governmental body

____ I have public agency responsibility

____ I am a member of an interested private community organization

____ I have an industrial or commercial interest in the Study's recommendations

____ I have a personal interest, but am not affiliated with any of the above

5. Are you a member of the Citizen Advisory Committee or the Regional Scientific Task Force?

____ Yes   ____ No

6. Are you a member of a Basin Advisory Committee?

____ Yes   ____ No

7. Do you hold an elective or appointed office in government?

____ Yes   ____ No

If "yes," at what level?

____ Town   ____ State

____ City   ____ Federal

____ County/Regional

8. What is your educational background?

____ High school or less   ____ Graduate work

____ Some college or college degree

9. What is your approximate family income?

____ Under $8,500   ____ $13,000–$20,000

____ $8,500–$13,000   ____ Over $20,000

10. Have you read the summary of the SENE Report "How to Guide Growth in Southeastern New England"?

____ All of it   ____ None of it

____ Part of it   ____ I never received or saw a copy

11. Have you seen and/or read a copy of the full Report of the Study?
    ____ Yes   ____ No
    If "yes," where?
    ____ Town hall   ____ I received one in the mail
    ____ Local library   ____ Someone else showed it to
                                       me

12. Have you ever personally discussed the Southeastern New England Study with a member of its Citizen Advisory Committee?
    ____ Yes   ____ No

13. Have you ever personally discussed the Southeastern New England Study with a member of its staff?
    ____ Yes   ____ No

14. Which of the following has most influenced your opinions on the SENE Study? (Most Important = 1, Second Most Important = 2, etc.)
    ____ Newspaper, radio or T.V. coverage
    ____ Public meeting presentations
    ____ Personal contacts with SENE Study Advisory Committee members
    ____ Personal contacts with the Study's staff
    ____ Knowledge of the problems discussed in the Study

15. Do you feel that you know enough about the Study to be able to offer comments at tonight's meeting?
    ____ Yes   ____ No

16. Do you feel that you have had an adequate opportunity to express your opinions regarding the Southeastern New England Study's Report?
    ____ Yes   ____ No

17. Do you feel that the Southeastern New England Study has considered the opinions expressed at previous public meetings (if you attended any)?
    ____ Yes   ____ No   ____ To some extent

18. Does the SENE Report sufficiently reflect the needs and preferences of your community?
    ____ Yes   ____ No   ____ To some extent

19. Planning decisions concerning the use of land and water resources should be made primarily at the
    ____ Local level   ____ Local level with broad state
    ____ Regional level   guidelines
    ____ State level   ____ Federal level
    ____ Inter-state level

20. What is your general opinion of the Report produced by the South-eastern New England Study?

____ Very much approve   ____ Disapprove

____ Approve   ____ Very much disapprove

____ Undecided

21. In which of the following concerns are you the *most* interested?

____ Environmental concerns

____ Industrial or commercial concerns

____ Concerns for private property

____ Concerns for community betterment

____ Recreational concerns

22. Do you feel that the Study's recommendations will be affected by the opinions expressed tonight?

____ Yes   ____ No   ____ To some extent

Optional Comments:

Works Cited

Books, Articles, and Reports

Allison, Graham T. *The Essence of Decision: Explaining the Cuban Missile Crisis.* Boston, Little, Brown, 1971.

Almond, Gabriel A., and Sidney Verba. *The Civic Culture.* Princeton, Princeton University Press, 1963.

Appleby, Paul. *Policy and Administration.* University, Ala., University of Alabama Press, 1949.

Arnstein, Sherry R. "A Ladder of Citizen Participation." *Journal of the American Institute of Planners,* 35 (1969), 216–24.

Bachrach, Peter. *The Theory of Democratic Elitism: A Critique.* Boston, Little, Brown, 1967.

Banfield, Edward C. *The Unheavenly City Revisited.* Boston, Little, Brown, 1974.

Berger, Bernard B. "Citizen Participation in Comprehensive River Basin Planning." Printed in the *Federal Register,* Tuesday, December 21, 1971, Vol. 36, No. 245, Part II. Presented at the Conservation Foundation's Environmental Forum, Washington, D.C., March 9, 1972.

Bishop, Bruce A. *Structuring Communications Programs for Public Participation in Water Resources Planning.* Ft. Belvoir, Va., U.S. Army Corps of Engineers, Institute for Water Resources, May 1975.

Borton, Thomas E., Katherine P. Warner, and William J. Wenrich. *The Susquehanna Communication-Participation Study.* Ft. Belvoir, Va., U.S. Army Corps of Engineers, Institute for Water Resources, IWR Report 70-6, December 1970.

Brown, David S. "The Management of Advisory Committees: An Assessment for the 1970's." *Public Administration Review,* 32 (1972), 334–42.

Bureau of Land Management. "Public Participation in the Environmental Assessment Process: Training Session Notebook." Washington, D.C., 1974.

Citizens' Advisory Committee on Environmental Quality. *Report to the President and to the Council on Environmental Quality*. Washington, D.C., December 1975.

Coates, Joseph F. "Why Public Participation Is Essential in Technology Assessment." *Public Administration Review*, 35 (1975), 67–69.

Cole, Richard L. *Citizen Participation and the Urban Policy Process*. Lexington, Mass., D. C. Heath, 1974.

Congressional Record. December 20, 1969, p. 2., Document No. 2.

Congressional Record. July 9, 1969, pp. 71, 74.

Congressional Record. October 8, 1969, pp. 20, 23.

Connecticut River Basin Coordinating Committee. *Connecticut River Basin Comprehensive Water and Related Land Resources Investigation*. October 1970.

Curran, Terence P. "Water Resources Management in the Public Interest." *Water Resources Bulletin*, 7 (1971), 33–39.

Dahlgren, Charles W. *Public Participation in Water Resources Planning: A Multi-Media Course*. Professional Development Paper 72-1. Ft. Belvoir, Va., U.S. Army Corps of Engineers, Institute for Water Resources, April 1972.

Davidoff, Paul. "Working toward Redistributive Justice." *Journal of the American Institute of Planners*, 41 (1975), 317–18.

Delli Priscoli, Jerry. "Citizen Advisory Groups and Conflict Resolution in Regional Water Resources Planning." *Water Resources Bulletin*, 11 (1975), 1233–43.

———. *Public Participation in Regional Level B Water Resources Planning: A Preliminary View*. Washington, D.C., Water Resources Council, Special Consulting Report, October 1974.

Derthick, Martha. *Between State and Nation: Regional Organizations of the United States*. Washington, D.C., Brookings Institution, 1974.

Dixon, John. "How Can Public Participation Become Real?" *Public Administration Review*, 35 (1975), 69–70.

Doerksen, Harvey R., and John C. Pierce. "Citizen Influence in Water Policy Decisions: Context, Constraints, and Alternatives." *Water Resources Bulletin*, 11 (1975), 953–64.

Douglas, William O. "The Corps of Engineers: The Public Be Damned!" In Walt Anderson, ed., *Politics and Environment*. Pacific Palisades, Calif., Goodyear Publishing Co., 1970, pp. 268–84.

Drew, Elizabeth B. "Dam Outrage: The Story of the Army Engineers." In Stephen E. Ambrose and James A. Barber, Jr., eds., *The Military and American Society*. New York, Free Press, 1972, pp. 274–95.

Dye, Thomas R. *Understanding Public Policy*. 2nd ed., Englewood Cliffs, N.J., Prentice-Hall, 1975.

Dynes, Russell R., and Dennis Wenger. "Factors in the Community Perception of Water Resource Problems." *Water Resources Bulletin,* 7 (1971), 644–51.

Elazar, Daniel J. *American Federalism: A View from the States.* New York, Thomas Crowell, 1972.

Environmental Protection Agency. "Public Participation in EPA's Water Pollution Control Activities: EPA Guidelines." In EPA's *Managing the Environment,* Washington, D.C. (1973), pp. 162–67.

Ertel, Madge O. *The Role of Citizen Advisory Groups in Water Resources Planning.* Amherst, Mass., Water Resources Research Center, University of Massachusetts, August 1974.

Ertel, Madge O., and Stuart G. Koch. *Citizen Participation in Comprehensive Water Resources Planning.* Amherst, Mass., Water Resources Research Center, University of Massachusetts, August 1976.

———. *Public Participation in Water Resources Planning: A Case Study and Literature Review.* Amherst, Mass., Water Resources Research Center, University of Massachusetts, July 1977.

"Executive Order 11514; Protection and Enhancement of Environmental Quality." March 5, 1970. In *Environmental Quality: Third Annual Report of the Council on Environmental Quality.* Washington, D.C. (1972), Appendix D.

Fantini, Mario, Marilyn Gittell, and Richard Magat. *Community Control and the Urban School.* New York, Praeger, 1970.

Flathman, Richard. *The Public Interest.* New York, John Wiley and Sons, 1966.

Frauenglass, Harvey. "Environmental Policy: Public Participation and the Open Information System." *Natural Resources Journal,* 11 (1971), 489–96.

Frederickson, H. George. "Organizational Theory and the New Public Administration." In Fred A. Kramer, ed., *Perspectives on Public Administration.* Cambridge, Mass., Winthrop Publishers (1973), pp. 185–200.

Fredrich, Augustine J. "Public Participation—Poison, Placebo, or Panacea." Unpublished paper presented at the ASCE Specialty Conference on "A Better Life through Water Resources Planning and Management," Fort Collins, Colorado, July 9–11, 1975.

Fried, Robert C. *Performance in American Bureaucracy.* Boston, Little, Brown, 1976.

Friedrich, Carl J. *Man and His Government.* New York, McGraw-Hill, 1963.

———. "Public Policy and the Nature of Administrative Responsibility." Reprinted in Francis Rourke, ed., *Bureaucratic Power in National Politics.* 2nd ed., Boston, Little, Brown (1972), pp. 316–25.

Fritschler, A. Lee. *Smoking and Politics: Policymaking and the Federal*

Bureaucracy. 2nd ed., Englewood Cliffs, N.J., Prentice-Hall, 1975.

Gallagher, Dorothy. "The Collapse of the Great Teton Dam." *New York Times Magazine,* September 19, 1976, pp. 16, 95–103, 108.

Geerdes, Jenene. "Communications Aspects of the Long Island Sound Study." Unpublished Master's Thesis, Graduate School of Corporate and Political Communication, Fairfield University, June 1975.

Gittell, Marilyn. *Participants and Participation.* New York, Praeger, 1967.

Goodman, Robert. *After the Planners.* New York, Simon and Schuster, 1973.

Green, Mark J., James M. Fallows, and David R. Zwick. *Who Runs Congress?* New York, Bantam Books, 1972.

Gregorka, David A. *The Citizen Participation Program of the Maumee River Basin Level B Study.* Ann Arbor, Mich., Water Resources Management Program, University of Michigan, 1974.

Halper, Thomas. *Foreign Policy Crisis: Appearance and Reality in Decision Making.* Columbus, Ohio, Charles E. Merrill, 1971.

Hanchey, James R. *Public Involvement in the Corps of Engineers Planning Process.* Ft. Belvoir, Va., U.S. Army Corps of Engineers, Institute for Water Resources, IWR Report 75-R4, October 1975.

Harris, Joseph P. *Congressional Control of Administration.* Washington, D.C., Brookings Institution, 1964.

Hart, David K. "Theories of Government Related to Decentralization and Citizen Participation." *Public Administration Review,* 32 (1972), 603–21.

Hoggan, Daniel H., et al. *A Study of the Effectiveness of Water Resources Planning Groups: A Final Report.* Logan, Utah, Utah Water Research Laboratory, Utah State University, March 1974.

Ingram, Helen. "Patterns of Politics in Water Resources Development." *Natural Resources Journal,* 11 (1971), 102–118.

Ittner, Ruth, and Dorothee S. Pealy. "Citizen Participation; Search for Criteria." *Washington Public Policy Notes,* Institute of Governmental Research, University of Washington, Seattle, Wash., 5 (1977).

James, L. Douglas. "Formulation of Nonstructural Flood Control Programs." *Water Resources Bulletin,* 11 (1975), 688–705.

Kahle, R., and R. L. Lee. *A Q-Methodological Study of Attitudes toward Water Resources and Implications for Using Mass Media in Dissemination of Water Research Results.* Columbia, Mo., Water Resources Research Center, University of Missouri, 1974.

Katznelson, Ira, and Mark Kesselman. *The Politics of Power.* New York, Harcourt, Brace, Jovanovich, 1975.

Kaufman, Herbert. "Administrative Decentralization and Political Power." *Public Administration Review,* 29 (1969), 3–15.

Keene, John, and Ann Louise Strong. "The Brandywine Plan." *Journal of the American Institute of Planners,* 35 (1970), 50–58.

Koelzer, Victor A. "A Proposed National Organizational Structure for Water Resources Planning." *Water Resources Bulletin*, 9 (1973), 167–80.

Kotler, Milton. *Neighborhood Government: The Local Foundation of Political Life*. Indianapolis, Bobbs-Merrill, 1969.

Lambright, William H. *Governing Science and Technology*. New York, Oxford University Press, 1976.

Lane, Robert E. *Political Ideology*. New York, Free Press, 1962.

League of Women Voters' Educational Fund. *The Big Water Fight*. Brattleboro, Vt., Stephen Greene Press, 1966.

Long, Norton. *The Polity*. Chicago, Rand McNally, 1962.

Maass, Arthur. "Congress and Water Resources." In Francis Rourke, ed., *Bureaucratic Power in National Politics*. 2nd ed., Boston, Little, Brown (1972), pp. 139–52.

Mainzer, Lewis C. *Political Bureaucracy*. Glenview, Ill., Scott, Foresman, 1973.

Mazmanian, Daniel A. "Citizens and the Assessment of Technology: An Examination of the Participation Thesis." Paper prepared for delivery at the 1974 annual meeting of the American Political Science Association, Palmer House, Chicago, Ill., August 29–September 2, 1974.

Mazmanian, Daniel A., and Mordecai Lee. "Tradition Be Damned! The Army Corps of Engineers Is Changing." *Public Administration Review*, 35 (1975), 166–72.

Milbrath, Lester W. *An Extra Dimension of Representation in Water Resources Planning: A Survey Study of Erie and Niagara Counties*. Buffalo, State University of New York, 1976.

Miller, S. M., and Martin Rein. "Participation, Poverty and Administration." *Public Administration Review*, 29 (1969), 15–25.

Mogulof, Melvin B. *Citizen Participation: The Local Perspective*. Washington, D.C., Urban Institute, March 1970.

Moreell, Ben. *Our Nation's Water Resources—Policies and Politics*. Chicago, Law School of University of Chicago, 1956.

Morley, C. G. "Public Participation: A Right to Decide." In Agassiz Center for Water Studies, *The Allocative Conflicts in Water-Resource Management*. Winnipeg, University of Manitoba (1974), pp. 513–24.

Mosher, Frederick C. *Democracy and the Public Service*. New York, Oxford University Press, 1968.

Moynihan, Daniel P. *Maximum Feasible Misunderstanding: Community Action in the War on Poverty*. New York, Free Press, 1969.

Murphy, Walter F. "The Framework of Judicial Power." In Alan Shank, ed., *American Politics, Policies, and Priorities*. Boston, Holbrook Press (1974), pp. 348–60.

National Water Commission. *See* U.S. National Water Commission.

Nelson, Ron. "Level B Water Resources Planning in an Urban Setting." *Water Resources Bulletin*, 11 (1975), 605–12.

Neustadt, Richard E. *Presidential Power*. New York, John Wiley and Sons, 1960.

New York Times, February 18, 1977, pp. A-1 and B-7.

Ortolano, Leonard. *Water Resources Decision-Making on the Basis of the Public Interest*. Ft. Belvoir, Va., U.S. Army Corps of Engineers, Institute for Water Resources, February 1975.

Pateman, Carole. *Participation and Democratic Theory*. Cambridge, England, Cambridge University Press, 1970.

Paulette, R. G., and W. R. Klatt. "Water Resource Management-Planning for Action." *Water Resources Bulletin*, 10 (1974), 384–88.

Pitkin, Hanna. *The Concept of Representation*. Berkeley, University of California Press, 1967.

Powell, Norman J. *Responsible Public Bureaucracy in the United States*. Boston, Allyn and Bacon, 1967.

Ragan, James F. *Public Participation in Water Resources Planning: An Evaluation of the Programs of 15 Corps of Engineers Districts*. Ft. Belvoir, Va., U.S. Army Corps of Engineers, Institute for Water Resources, IWR Report 75-6, November 1975.

Reagan, Michael D. "Policy Issues: The Interaction of Substance and Process." *Polity*, 1 (1968), 35–51.

Report of the Citizens Review Committee of the Connecticut River Basin Comprehensive Water and Related Land Resources Investigation to the New England River Basins Commission. Boston, February 1, 1971.

Riedel, James A. "Citizen Participation: Myths and Realities." *Public Administration Review*, 32 (1972), 211–20.

Rourke, Francis E. *Bureaucracy, Politics, and Public Policy*. Boston, Little, Brown, 1969.

———. *Bureaucratic Power in National Politics*. 2nd ed., Boston, Little, Brown, 1972.

Sargent, Howard L. "Fishbowl Planning Immerses Pacific Northwest Citizens in Corps Projects." *Civil Engineering*, 42 (1972), 54–57.

Sax, Joseph L. *Defending the Environment: A Handbook for Citizen Action*. New York, Vintage Books, 1972.

Schultze, Charles E. *The Politics and Economics of Public Spending*. Washington, D.C., Brookings Institution, 1968.

Schumpeter, Joseph. *Capitalism, Socialism and Democracy*. New York, Harper and Row, 1962.

Selznick, Philip. *TVA and the Grass Roots*. Berkeley, University of California Press, 1949.

Shanley, Robert A. *Attitudes and Interactions of Citizen Advisory Groups and Governmental Officials in the Water Resources Planning Process*. Amherst, Mass., Water Resources Research Center, University of Massachusetts, August 1976.

Sharkansky, Ira. *Regionalism in American Politics*. Indianapolis, Bobbs-Merrill, 1970.

Strange, John H. "The Impact of Citizen Participation on Public Administration." *Public Administration Review*, 32 (1972), 457–70.

Thomas, Norman C. *Rule 9: Politics, Administration, and Civil Rights.* New York, Random House, 1966.

Tinkham, Lester A. "The Public's Role in Decision-Making for Federal Water Resources Development." *Water Resources Bulletin*, 10 (1974), 691–96.

Tucker, Richard C. "Planners as a 'Public' in Water Resources Public Participation Programs." *Water Resources Bulletin*, 8 (1972), 257–65.

United States Council on Environmental Quality. *Environmental Quality: Third Annual Report of the Council on Environmental Quality.* Washington, D.C., 1972.

———. "Preparation of Environmental Impact Statements—Guidelines." *Federal Register*, Vol. 38, No. 147, Part II, August 1, 1973, pp. 20,550–20,561.

United States House Committee on Merchant Marine and Fisheries. *Report on the Coastal Zone Management Act.* 92nd Congress, 2nd Session, House Report 92-1544, May 5, 1972.

United States National Water Commission. *Water Policies for the Future: Final Report.* Washington, D.C., Government Printing Office, June 1973.

United States Senate Commerce Committee. *Report on the Coastal Zone Management Act.* Report 92-753, 92nd Congress, 2nd Session, April 19, 1972.

United States Senate Committee on Public Works. *Report on the Federal Water Pollution Control Act Amendments of 1971.* 92nd Congress, 1st Session, Senate Report No. 92-414, October 28, 1971.

United States Senate. Hearings of the Subcommittee on Air and Water Pollution of the Committee on Public Works. 92nd Congress, 1st Session, March 18, 1971, in *Water Pollution Control Legislation—1971*, Part 2.

United States Senate. "Preserving the Future of Long Island Sound." *Hearings before the Subcommittee on Executive Reorganization and Government Research of the Committee on Government Operations*, on S.2472, Washington, D.C., Government Printing Office, 1970.

United States Water Resources Council. "Principles and Standard for Planning Water and Related Land Resources." *Federal Register*, Vol. 38, No. 174, Part III, September 10, 1973.

Wagner, Thomas R., and Leonard Ortolano, "Analysis of New Techniques for Public Involvement in Water Planning," *Water Resources Bulletin*, 11 (1975), 329–44.

Warner, Katherine P. *Public Participation in Water Resources Planning.* Arlington, Va., National Water Commission, July 1971.

Wengert, Norman. "Where Can We Go with Public Participation in the Planning Process?" In *Social and Economic Aspects of Water Re-*

sources Development: Proceedings of the 1971 National Symposium of the American Water Resources Association, Ithaca, New York, June 21–23, 1971, pp. 9–17.

Widditsch, Ann. Public Workshops on the Puget Sound and Adjacent Waters Study: An Evaluation. Ft. Belvoir, Va., U.S. Army Corps of Engineers, Institute for Water Resources, Report 72-2, June 1972.

Wildavsky, Aaron. The Politics of the Budgetary Process. Boston, Little, Brown, 1964.

Wilson, Raymond H. Toward a Philosophy of Planning: Attitudes of Federal Water Planners. EPA Report No. R5-73-015. Washington, D.C., Government Printing Office, 1973.

Woll, Peter. American Bureaucracy. 2nd ed., New York, W. W. Norton, 1977.

Wolff, Robert D. Involving the Public and the Hierarchy in Corps of Engineers' Survey Investigations. Stanford, Calif., Dept. of Civil Engineering, Report EEP-45, Stanford University, 1971.

NERBC Publications and Study Documents

Connecticut River Basin Program. "Comments on The River's Reach: 90-day Public Review Draft Report and Environmental Impact Statement." July 1976.

———. Local Perspectives on Flood Management Planning in the Connecticut River Basin: Report on Phase 2 Local Meetings. November 30, 1974.

———. "Memorandum." August 10, 1973.

———. "Memorandum from the SAG Chairman; SAG's Mission and Effectiveness." July 5, 1973.

———. "Reports on the CAG and SAG Meetings."

———. "The River's Reach: A Plan for Flood Damage Reduction and Flood Plain Management in the Connecticut River Basin; 90 Day Public Review Draft." December 1975.

Dakin, Janet W. (Chair, CRBP Public Information Committee). "Report to the CAG on the Phase One Forums." December 14, 1973.

Long Island Sound Study. "CAC Comments on the LISS Draft Plan." CAC Memorandum No. 75-15, February 15, 1975.

———. Citizen Advisory Committee. "Goals for the Region." CAC Memorandum No. 74-14. November 1973.

———. Citizen Advisory Committee. Memorandum No. 74-16. November 27, 1973.

———. Citizen Advisory Committee. Memorandum. October 5, 1975.

———. Memorandum No. 75-27 from Frank Gregg, chairman of NERBC. April 11, 1975.

———. "Minutes of the CAC Meetings."

————. "Minutes and Prepared Statements of Public Meetings." January 1975.

————. "Minutes of the R/PAC Meetings."

————. "People and the Sound: Draft Main Report of the Long Island Sound Regional Study. November 1974.

————. "Report of the Public Workshops of May/June 1973." August 21, 1973 (draft), and October 19, 1973 (final).

————. "Results of the Opinion Poll Conducted by the Long Island Sound Regional Study." July 9, 1974.

————. "Selected Newsclips of the Spring 1974 Public Meetings." May 31, 1974.

————. "People and the Sound: A Plan for Long Island Sound." November 1974. In *Urban Sea*. Earlier issues appeared in summer 1973, fall 1973, and spring 1974.

McHugh, J. L., and H. M. Austin. "Prospects for Managing the Fisheries of Long Island Sound." Unpublished paper presented at December 1973, R/PAC Seminar, sponsored by LISS.

New England River Basins Commission. *1975 Annual Report*. Boston, 1975.

————. *The NERBC 1980 Connecticut River Basin Plan: New England River Basins Commission Findings and Recommendations on the Connecticut River Basin Comprehensive Water and Related Land Resources Investigation*. Boston, January 1, 1972.

————. *People and the Sound: Land Use*. Boston, 1975.

————. *People and the Sound: Marine Transportation*. Boston, 1975.

————. *People and the Sound: A Plan for Long Island Sound; Vol. 1, Summary; Vol. 2, Supplement; and Ten Planning Reports*. Boston, July 1975.

————. *Plan of Study: Long Island Sound Regional Study*. Boston, August 1, 1971.

————. *Report of the Southeastern New England Study: Summary, Regional Report (with Environmental Statement), and Ten Planning Area Reports*. Boston, December 1975.

————. "SENE and the Connecticut River Diversions." Memorandum of July 29, 1975.

————. *The River's Reach: A Unified Program for Flood Plain Management in the Connecticut River Basin*. Boston, December 1976. Published version of draft listed above.

————. *Southeastern New England Water and Related Land Resources Study: Plan of Study*. Boston, April 1972.

————. "A State–Federal Partnership" (undated pamphlet).

Southeastern New England Study. "Citizen Preferences for Solutions." Sent with a Memorandum to SMT, May 24, 1974.

———. "Goals and Objectives for the Southeastern New England Study." Memorandum from the CAC and R/STF. May 1974.

———. "How to Guide Growth in Southeastern New England: Report of the Southeastern New England Water and Related Land Resources Study," Review Draft, May 1975.

———. "How to Guide Growth in Southeastern New England: A Management Proposal for Public Discussion." May 1975.

———. "Minutes of the Quarterly Meetings of CAC and R/STF."

———. "Minutes of the Third Series of Public Workshops Commenting on the 90 Day Review Draft." May/June 1975.

———. "Progress Report; September 1972 to September 1973." 1973.

———. "Public Meeting Summaries." May/June 1975.

———. "Report of the Interim Citizens Advisory Committee." 1971.

Notes

Introduction

1. "Bureaucrat" is used throughout merely to designate individuals who work in the American public service, and is synonymous with such other terms as "public administrator." Although many people use the word pejoratively, that connotation is not intended here.

2. Herbert Kaufman, "Administrative Decentralization and Political Power," *Public Administration Review*, 29 (1969), 3–15. Norman J. Powell, *Responsible Public Bureaucracy in the United States* (Boston, Allyn and Bacon, 1967).

3. Marilyn Gittell, *Participants and Participation* (New York, Praeger, 1967). Mario Fantini, Marilyn Gittell, and Richard Magat, *Community Control and the Urban School* (New York, Praeger, 1970).

4. Hanna Pitkin, *The Concept of Representation* (Berkeley, University of California Press, 1967).

5. Ibid., pp. 55–59.

1. Problems in Water Resources Planning

1. Thomas R. Dye usefully defines a public policy as "whatever governments choose to do or not to do." See Thomas R. Dye, *Understanding Public Policy*, 2nd ed. (Englewood Cliffs, N.J., Prentice-Hall, 1975), p. 1.

2. Numerous examples may be found in Edward C. Banfield, *The Unheavenly City Revisited* (Boston, Little, Brown, 1974), esp. chap. 1.

3. Lewis C. Mainzer, *Political Bureaucracy* (Glenview, Ill., Scott, Foresman, 1973), p. 40.

4. Francis E. Rourke, *Bureaucracy, Politics, and Public Policy* (Boston, Little, Brown, 1969), p. 50.

5. Carl J. Friedrich, "Public Policy and the Nature of Administrative Responsibility," rep. in Francis Rourke, ed., *Bureaucratic Power in National Politics*, 2nd ed. (Boston, Little, Brown, 1972), p. 318.

6. Peter Woll, *American Bureaucracy*, 2nd ed. (New York, W. W. Norton, 1977), p. 185.

7. Ibid., pp. 195–96.

8. Norman C. Thomas, *Rule 9: Politics, Administration, and Civil Rights* (New York, Random House, 1966), p. 6.

9. Mainzer, pp. 11–13, 68.

10. Frederick C. Mosher, *Democracy and the Public Service* (New York, Oxford University Press, 1968), p. 3.

11. Harvey R. Doerksen and John C. Pierce, "Citizen Influence in Water Policy Decisions: Context, Constraints, and Alternatives," *Water Resources Bulletin*, 11 (1975), 961.

12. For a different view see Norton Long, *The Polity* (Chicago, Rand McNally, 1962), p. 70. Long concludes that because bureaucrats are more demographically representative of the public than are most elected officials, policies created by administrators, rather than by these other officials, will more accurately reflect public needs and preferences. However, the still limited nature of the demographic representation present in most agencies, and the lack of documentation concerning the linkages he suggests, temper the optimism that may be derived from Long's thesis.

13. As Friedrich observes, the problem is that "administrative responsibility has not kept pace with our administrative tasks" (p. 319).

14. For further discussion see A. Lee Fritschler, *Smoking and Politics: Policymaking and the Federal Bureaucracy*, 2nd ed. (Englewood Cliffs, N.J.: Prentice-Hall, 1975). Most studies of Congress make basically the same observation in studying the law-making process. See Mark J. Green, James M. Fallows, and David R. Zwick, *Who Runs Congress?* (New York, Bantam Books, 1972), chap. 2.

15. Graham T. Allison, *The Essence of Decision: Explaining the Cuban Missile Crisis* (Boston, Little, Brown, 1971), p. 144.

16. Rourke, pp. 106–7.

17. Ibid., pp. 114–15.

18. Joseph F. Coates, "Why Public Participation Is Essential in Technology Assessment," *Public Administration Review*, 35 (1975), 67.

19. Mosher, p. 122.

20. Robert Goodman, *After the Planners* (New York, Simon and Schuster, 1973), p. 12.

21. Mosher, p. 108.

22. Allison, p. 166.

23. For a concise discussion of representative bureaucracy, see Mainzer, pp. 126–32.

24. Robert C. Fried, *Performance in American Bureaucracy* (Boston, Little, Brown, 1976), p. 8.

25. Still others have sought to avoid such value-laden questions by focusing primarily on the processes by which policies are created. For amplification, see Dye, p. 2.

26. As Powell notes, the term itself reflects the different roots of American public administration. For amplification, see Powell, pp. 6–7.

27. Fried, pp. 44–45.

28. Rourke, p. 3.

29. For further discussion see Richard Flathman, *The Public Interest* (New

York, John Wiley and Sons, 1966), p. 41. Flathman's standard is that the consequences for all members of the society must be considered.

30. Michael D. Reagan, "Policy Issues: The Interaction of Substance and Process," *Polity*, 1 (1968), 47.

31. It should be noted that Fried uses three comparable criteria, "effectiveness," "responsiveness," and "liberalism," although I arrived at the above standards independently.

32. Rourke, pp. 3–6.

33. Lester A. Tinkham, "The Public's Role in Decision-Making for Federal Water Resources Development," *Water Resources Bulletin*, 10 (1974), 692.

34. In fact, the vast majority of the projects opposed by the Carter Administration during its first two years have continued to receive Congressional support.

35. Fried, p. 112.

36. Elizabeth B. Drew, "Dam Outrage: The Story of the Army Engineers," in Stephen E. Ambrose and James A. Barber, Jr., eds., *The Military and American Society* (New York, Free Press, 1972), pp. 279, 282.

37. William O. Douglas, "The Corps of Engineers: The Public Be Damned," in Walt Anderson, ed., *Politics and Environment* (Pacific Palisades, Calif., Goodyear Publishing Co., 1970), p. 282.

38. U.S. National Water Commission, *Water Policies for the Future: Final Report* (Washington, D.C., Government Printing Office, 1973), p. 389. For a more general discussion, see also Arthur Maass, "Congress and Water Resources," in Rourke, ed., *Bureaucratic Power in National Politics*, 2nd ed. (Boston, Little, Brown, 1972), pp. 139–52.

39. From a statement by Harold Arthur of the Bureau's Denver office. Dorothy Gallagher, "The Collapse of the Great Teton Dam," *New York Times Magazine*, September 19, 1976, p. 103.

40. National Water Commission, p. 389.

41. Gallagher, pp. 95–103.

42. Ibid., pp. 95–96.

43. Russell R. Dynes and Dennis Wenger, "Factors in the Community Perception of Water Resource Problems," *Water Resources Bulletin*, 7 (1971), 644–51.

44. For another example see Charles E. Schultze, *The Politics and Economics of Public Spending* (Washington, D.C., Brookings Institution, 1968), p. 3. Schultze indicates that it would seem to be easier to quantify decision-making in the realm of military or defense policies than in many other substantive areas.

45. Drew, p. 280.

46. Ibid., p. 281.

47. National Water Commission, p. 407.

48. Daniel H. Hoggan, et al., *A Study of the Effectiveness of Water Resources Planning Groups: A Final Report* (Logan, Utah, Utah Water Research Laboratory, Utah State University, March 1974), p. 26.

49. Ibid., p. 30. For an examination of survey research in this area see Raymond H. Wilson, *Toward a Philosophy of Planning: Attitudes of Federal Water Planners*, EPA Report No. R5-73-015 (Washington, D.C., Government Printing Office, 1973).

50. To examine similar criticisms levied at the planning profession as a whole,

see Paul Davidoff, "Working toward Redistributive Justice," *Journal of the American Institute of Planners*, 41 (1975), 317–18. Authors like Davidoff seek to integrate social concerns, especially for "redistributive justice," into planning activities.

51. Douglas, p. 272.

52. Joseph P. Harris, *Congressional Control of Administration* (Washington, D.C., Brookings Institution, 1964).

53. Powell, p. 70.

54. National Water Commission, chaps. 9, 10.

55. Richard E. Neustadt, *Presidential Power* (New York, John Wiley and Sons, 1960), pp. 33–37.

56. Walter F. Murphy, "The Framework of Judicial Power," in Alan Shank, ed., *American Politics, Policies, and Priorities* (Boston, Holbrook Press, 1974), p. 352.

57. Ibid.

58. Joseph L. Sax, *Defending the Environment: A Handbook for Citizen Action* (New York, Vintage Books, 1972), pp. 131–35.

59. Friedrich, p. 320.

60. H. George Frederickson, "Organizational Theory and the New Public Administration," in Fred. A. Kramer, ed., *Perspectives on Public Administration* (Cambridge, Mass., Winthrop Publishers, 1973), p. 196.

61. Mainzer, pp. 132–35.

62. Kaufman, p. 3.

63. See Sherry A. Arnstein, "A Ladder of Citizen Participation," *Journal of the American Institute of Planners*, 35 (1969), 217. Arnstein's "ladder" provides a concise summary of the many ways in which citizens can be involved in administrative policy-making.

64. Although one can say that citizens participate in politics in many ways— by voting, by joining or working for parties or interest groups, and by writing letters to public officials—the terms public and citizen participation and citizen involvement are used interchangeably hereafter for efforts to involve citizens directly in administrative activities.

2. The Rationale and the Experience

1. A different version of this chapter first appeared in Madge O. Ertel and Stuart G. Koch, *Public Participation in Water Resources Planning: A Case Study and Literature Review* (Amherst, Mass., Water Resources Research Center, University of Massachusetts, July 1977).

2. Daniel P. Moynihan, *Maximum Feasible Misunderstanding: Community Action in the War on Poverty* (New York, Free Press, 1969). See also John Strange, "The Impact of Citizen Participation on Public Administration," *Public Administration Review*, 32 (1972), 457–70.

3. Two notable exceptions to this statement are by David Hart and Norman Wengert. See Hart, "Theories of Government Related to Decentralization and Citizen Participation," *Public Administration Review*, 32 (1972), pp. 603–21, and Wengert, "Where Can We Go with Public Participation in the Planning Process?" *Social and Economic Aspects of Water Resources Development: Proceedings of the 1971 National Symposium of the American Water Resources Association* (Ithaca, New York, June 21–23, 1971), pp. 10–11.

4. For a related discussion, see Doerksen and Pierce, p. 956.

5. Though not all these arguments are directly related to the concern for bureaucratic accountability, for a more complete view of the concept it is necessary to consider all five.

6. Richard L. Cole, *Citizen Participation and the Urban Policy Process* (Lexington, Mass., D. C. Heath, 1974), p. 2.

7. Ibid.

8. Ibid., p. 3.

9. See Carole Pateman, *Participation and Democratic Theory* (Cambridge, England, Cambridge University Press, 1970).

10. Ira Katznelson and Mark Kesselman, *The Politics of Power* (New York, Harcourt, Brace, Jovanovich, 1975), pp. 19–32.

11. Peter Bachrach, *The Theory of Democratic Elitism: A Critique* (Boston, Little, Brown, 1967), pp. 95, 98.

12. Pateman, p. 46.

13. Cole, p. 6.

14. For example, James urges planners who are developing a nonstructural flood control program to select alternative measures shown to be acceptable to citizens in the communities in question. See L. Douglas James, "Formulation of Nonstructural Flood Control Programs," *Water Resources Bulletin*, 11 (1975), 705.

15. The League of Women Voters' Educational Fund, *The Big Water Fight* (Brattleboro, Vt., Stephen Greene Press, 1966), p. 120.

16. Katherine P. Warner, *Public Participation in Water Resources Planning* (Arlington, Va., National Water Commission, July 1971), p. 35. For a discussion of the need for planners to take into account sociopolitical realities, see R. G. Paulette and W. R. Klatt, "Water Resource Management-Planning for Action," *Water Resources Bulletin*, 10 (1974), 386–87.

17. Harvey Frauenglass, "Environmental Policy: Public Participation and the Open Information System," *Natural Resources Journal*, 11 (1971), 489.

18. Richard Tucker notes that standards related to such concerns as environmental quality are inherently "perception-oriented"—that is, highly dependent on "intangibles and personal value preferences." See Richard C. Tucker, "Planners as a 'Public' in Water Resources Public Participation Programs," *Water Resources Bulletin*, 8 (1972), 261.

19. See Milton Kotler, *Neighborhood Government: The Local Foundation of Political Life* (Indianapolis, Bobbs-Merrill, 1969).

20. Pateman, p. 110.

21. Gabriel A. Almond and Sidney Verba, *The Civic Culture* (Princeton, Princeton University Press, 1963), pp. 46, 47, 297–99.

22. Mainzer, p. 139. Cole, p. 10.

23. James A. Riedel, "Citizen Participation: Myths and Realities," *Public Administration Review*, 32 (1972), 213.

24. For a discussion of anomie, see Robert E. Lane, *Political Ideology* (New York, Free Press, 1962), p. 407.

25. Ibid., pp. 407–8.

26. Daniel A. Mazmanian, "Citizens and the Assessment of Technology: An Examination of the Participation Thesis," a paper prepared for delivery at the 1974 annual meeting of the American Political Science Association, Chicago, August 29–September 2, 1974, pp. 39–40.

27. Jerry Delli Priscoli, "Citizen Advisory Groups and Conflict Resolution in Regional Water Resources Planning," *Water Resources Bulletin*, 11 (1975), 1241.

28. For example, Mazmanian argues that the Corps of Engineers embraced the concept of participation in the early 1970's largely to gain support for its projects. Mazmanian, pp. 2–3, 34–35.

29. For further discussion, see Mainzer, p. 141.

30. For a discussion of Bernard Berelson's thesis, see Pateman, p. 7. For amplification, see Joseph Schumpeter, *Capitalism, Socialism and Democracy* (New York, Harper and Row, 1962), p. 262.

31. For a concise discussion of Dahl's views, see Pateman, p. 10.

32. S. M. Miller and Martin Rein, "Participation, Poverty and Administration," *Public Administration Review*, 29 (1969), 15–25.

33. Augustine J. Fredrich, "Public Participation—Poison, Placebo, or Panacea," unpublished paper presented at the ASCE Specialty Conference on "A Better Life through Water Resources Planning and Management" at Fort Collins, Colorado, July 9–11, 1975, p. 5.

34. Bernard B. Berger, "Citizen Participation in Comprehensive River Basin Planning," printed in the *Federal Register*, Tuesday, December 21, 1971, Vol. 36, No. 245, Part II; presented at the Conservation Foundation's Environmental Forum, Washington, D.C., March 9, 1972, pp. 12–13.

35. Frauenglass, p. 489.

36. Gallagher, pp. 16, 98, 108.

37. See Philip Selznick, *TVA and the Grass Roots* (Berkeley, University of California Press, 1949).

38. See Moynihan, pp. 75–101.

39. Bureau of Land Management, "Public Participation in the Environmental Assessment Process: Training Session Notebook" (Washington, D.C., 1974), p. 14.

40. NEPA: Public Law 91-190 (42 USC 4321 et seq.). FWPCA: Public Law 92-500, October 18, 1972 (86 STAT. 817). CZM Act: Public Law 92-583, October 27, 1972 (86 STAT. 1280).

41. U.S. House Committee on Merchant Marine and Fisheries, *Report on the Coastal Zone Management Act*, 92nd Congress, 2nd Session, House Report 92-1544, May 5, 1972. U.S. Senate, Commerce Committee, *Report on the Coastal Zone Management Act*, Senate Report 92-753, 92nd Congress, 2nd Session, April 19, 1972.

42. Sydney Howe, Statement, Hearing of the Subcommittee on Air and Water Pollution, Committee on Public Works, U.S. Senate, 92nd Congress, 1st Session, March 18, 1971 (S 641), *Water Pollution Control Legislation—1971*, Part 2, p. 624.

43. *Congressional Record*, July 9, 1969, pp. 71, 74, quoted in Bureau of Land Management (note 39 above), pp. 10–11.

44. *Congressional Record*, December 20, 1969, p. 2, Document No. 2, quoted in Bureau of Land Management, pp. 12–13.

45. *Congressional Record*, October 8, 1969, pp. 20, 23, quoted in Bureau of Land Management, pp. 13–16.

46. U.S. Senate Committee on Public Works, *Report on the Federal Water Pollution Control Act Amendments of 1971*, 92nd Congress, 1st Session, Senate Report No. 92-414, October 28, 1971, p. 12.

47. C. G. Morley, "Public Participation: A Right to Decide," in Agassiz Center for Water Studies, *The Allocative Conflicts in Water-Resource Management* (Winnipeg, University of Manitoba, 1974), pp. 520–21.

48. Bruce A. Bishop, *Structuring Communications Programs for Public Participation in Water Resources Planning* (Ft. Belvoir, Va., U.S. Army Corps of Engineers, Institute for Water Resources, May 1975), p. 2.

49. Executive Order 11514, "Protection and Enhancement of Environmental Quality," March 5, 1970, in U.S. Council on Environmental Quality, *Environmental Quality: Third Annual Report of the Council on Environmental Quality* (Washington, D.C., 1972), Appendix D, p. 362.

50. U.S. Water Resources Council, "Principles and Standards for Planning Water and Related Land Resources," *Federal Register*, Vol. 38, No. 174, Part III, September 10, 1973. U.S. Council on Environmental Quality, "Preparation of Environmental Impact Statements—Guidelines," *Federal Register*, Vol. 38, No. 147, August 1, 1973, pp. 20,550—20,561. Environmental Protection Agency, "Public Participation in EPA's Water Pollution Control Activities: EPA Guidelines," in EPA's *Managing the Environment* (Washington, D.C., 1973), pp. 162–67.

51. Water Resources Council, pp. 24,785, 24,827 (pp. 13 and 96 of separate text).

52. Ibid., p. 24,827.

53. John Dixon, "How Can Public Participation become Real?" *Public Administration Review*, 35 (1975), 70.

54. In part this focus shows that a significant portion of the literature has been developed under the sponsorship of agencies like the Corps of Engineers, in need of information on developing and implementing strategies of public participation. For example, studies published by the U.S. Army Corps of Engineers, Institute for Water Resources, Ft. Belvoir, Va., include Bishop (note 48 above); Thomas E. Borton, Katherine P. Warner, and William J. Wenrich, *The Susquehanna Communication-Participation Study*, IWR Report 70-6 (December 1970); Charles W. Dahlgren, *Public Participation in Water Resources Planning: A Multi-Media Course*, Professional Development Paper 72-1 (April 1972); James R. Hanchey, *Public Involvement in the Corps of Engineers Planning Process*, IWR Report 75-R4 (October 1975); Leonard Ortolano, *Water Resources Decison-Making on the Basis of the Public Interest* (February 1975); James F. Ragan, *Public Participation in Water Resources Planning: An Evaluation of the Programs of 15 Corps of Engineers Districts*, IWR Report 75-6 (November 1975); and Ann Widditsch, *Public Workshops on the Puget Sound and Adjacent Waters Study: An Evaluation*, IWR Report 72-2 (June 1972).

55. For an example see John Keene and Ann Louise Strong, "The Brandywine Plan," *Journal of the American Institute of Planners*, 35 (1970), 50–58.

56. As reported by Wagner and Ortolano, some planners have also begun to employ computer-based modeling and simulation exercises. See Thomas R. Wagner and Leonard Ortolano, "Analysis of New Techniques for Public Involvement in Water Planning," *Water Resources Bulletin*, 11 (1975), 329–44.

57. Bishop, p. 52.

58. David S. Brown, "The Management of Advisory Committees: An Assessment for the 1970's," *Public Administration Review*, 32 (1972), 336.

59. Madge O. Ertel, *Citizen Advisory Groups in Water Resources Planning* (Amherst, Mass., Water Resources Research Center, University of Massachusetts, 1974), pp. 40–46.

60. Brown, pp. 340–41.

61. Howard L. Sargent, "Fishbowl Planning Immerses Pacific Northwest Citizens in Corps Projects," *Civil Engineering* 42 (1972), 54, 57.

62. Brown, pp. 340–41.

63. Widditsch (note 54 above).

64. Bishop, pp. 69–72.

65. R. Kahle and R. L. Lee, *A Q-Methodological Study of Attitudes toward Water Resources and Implications for Using Mass Media in Dissemination of Water Research Results* (Columbus, Mo., Water Resources Research Center, University of Missouri, 1974).

66. Sargent, pp. 54–57.

67. Hanchey (note 54 above), p. 22.

68. Wagner and Ortolano (note 56 above), pp. 340–42.

69. Ortolano (note 54 above), pp. 3–9, 3–10.

70. Warner (note 16 above), p. 23.

71. Ibid., p. 8.

72. For a discussion of how regional differences affect political behavior, see Ira Sharkansky, *Regionalism in American Politics* (Indianapolis, Bobbs-Merrill, 1970), chap. 3.

73. After surveying over 500 planning agencies, private organizations, and other groups, the Warner study recommended the use of advisory committees, informal contacts, and public meetings; see Warner, p. 14. For a different view, see Robert D. Wolff, *Involving the Public and the Hierarchy in Corps of Engineers Survey Investigations* (Stanford, Calif., Department of Civil Engineering, Report EEP-45, Stanford University, 1971).

3. Three Studies of Public Participation

1. For discussion see Victor A. Koelzer, "A Proposed National Organizational Structure for Water Resources Planning," *Water Resources Bulletin*, 9 (1973), 167–80.

2. Martha Derthick, *Between State and Nation: Regional Organizations of the United States* (Washington, D.C., Brookings Institution, 1974), chap. 4.

3. The scope of the NERBC was expanded to include the North Shore of Long Island to permit a comprehensive study of Long Island Sound.

4. New England River Basins Commission, *1975 Annual Report* (Boston, 1975), appendix D.

5. Ibid., p. 5.

6. Ibid., p. 10.

7. Ibid., p. 7.

8. Bishop (above, p. 167, note 48), p. 107.

9. See U.S. Senate, "Preserving the Future of Long Island Sound," *Hearings before the Subcommittee on Executive Reorganization and Government Research of the Committee on Government Operations*, on S.2472 (Washington, D.C., Government Printing Office, 1970).

10. NERBC, *Plan of Study: Long Island Sound Regional Study* (Boston, August 1, 1971).

11. NERBC, *Southeastern New England Water and Related Land Resources Study; Plan of Study* (Boston, April 1972).

12. Southeastern New England Study, "Report of the Interim Citizens Advisory Committee," 1971.

13. Connecticut River Basin Coordinating Committee, *Connecticut River Basin Comprehensive Water and Related Land Resources Investigation* (October 1970).

14. This quotation is from a letter to the author. For further information, see Berger (above, p. 166, note 34).

15. *Report of the Citizens Review Committee of the Connecticut River Basin Comprehensive Water and Related Land Resources Investigation to the New England River Basins Commission* (Boston, February 1, 1971).

16. NERBC, *The NERBC 1980 Connecticut River Basin Plan: New England River Basins Commission Findings and Recommendations on the Connecticut River Basin Comprehensive Water and Related Land Resources Investigation* (Boston, January 1, 1972).

17. Derthick, pp. 146, 155.

18. NERBC, *People and the Sound: A Plan for Long Island Sound, Vol. 2, Supplement* (Boston, July 1975), p. 19.

19. The timing of these meetings varied greatly. The CRBP Coordinating Group met less frequently than quarterly, and the Study Management Team met more frequently.

20. NERBC, *People and the Sound—Supplement*, p. 19.

21. The staffs had particular control over the legal and institutional portions of the studies.

22. From a telephone interview by Madge Ertel with Frank Gregg, Chairman of NERBC, July 1976.

23. For example, see Long Island Sound Study, Citizen Advisory Committee Memorandum, No. 74-16, November 27, 1973.

24. NERBC, *LISS Plan of Study*, p. 5-1.

25. Ibid.

26. Ibid., p. 6-1.

27. NERBC, *1980 Plan*, p. 125.

28. NERBC, *LISS Plan of Study*, p. 5-1.

29. NERBC, *SENE Plan of Study*, p. 6-3.

30. For further discussion, see NERBC, *LISS Plan of Study*, pp. 4-3 to 4-22.

31. In practice, the SENE staff invited the nonmember citizens who attended the CAC meetings to participate in the sessions.

32. SENE, "Interim CAC Report."

33. Ertel, p. 21.

34. NERBC, *LISS Plan of Study*, p. 5-3.

35. SENE, "Progress Report; September 1972 to September 1973," (1973).

36. Ertel, p. 40.

37. Ibid., pp. 34–36.

38. Ibid., pp. 29–32.

39. Ibid., p. 47.

40. From a letter to Madge O. Ertel from Roger Shope, Chairman of the LISS CAC.

41. Ertel, pp. 47, 55.

42. Ibid.

43. Ibid., pp. 47–48.

44. NERBC, *LISS Plan of Study*, pp. 5-2, 5-3. Ertel, p. 80.

45. LISS, Citizen Advisory Committee, "Goals for the Region," CAC Memorandum No. 74-14, November 1973; SENE, "Goals and Objectives for the Southeastern New England Study," Memorandum from CAC and R/STF, May 1974.

46. LISS, "Minutes of CAC Meeting No. 9," March 7, 1973, p. 2.

47. Ertel, p. 80.

48. For example, Janet W. Dakin (Chair, CRBP Public Information Committee), "Report to the CAG on the Phase One Forums," December 14, 1973, p. 1.

49. This concern was voiced by one CAC member at a LISS Coordinating Group Meeting on May 7, 1973, as well as at several CAC meetings.

50. Of the public officials who responded, 30.1 percent had discussed the studies with a CAC member, but only 16.9 percent of the respondents who were not officials had done so.

51. On several occasions R/PAC members discussed merging their activities with those of the CAC; several members argued, however, for a distinctly professional or scientific role in the study. They viewed their inputs as distinct from those of the lay citizens.

52. The Chairman of CRBP's SAG, Bernard Berger, in an interview with me in June 1976, indicated that he felt that science advisers could contribute more usefully in this manner than by attending group meetings, in part because of their busy schedules.

53. Letter from Professor Berger. These observations were expressed by him in the June 1976 interview also.

54. Ibid.

55. NERBC, *LISS Plan of Study*, pp. 6-3, 6-4. NERBC, *1980 Plan*, p. 126.

56. These figures appeared separately in various study materials and in CAC Minutes.

57. The original intent of the Basin Advisory Committees was therefore to generate participation on a subregional basis, but apart from two or three areas this strategy never developed.

58. Each staff employed a newsclip service to provide it with a complete record of all coverage in the area. These were studied by me and are the basis for these comments.

59. The *Boston Globe's* coverage of SENE's final meetings consisted in total of two news articles, one mention in a regular column, and two editorials; only one of the former gave the dates, times, and locations of the meetings. This did, however, appear on the first page of the "New England" section of the *Sunday Globe*. In other papers, the limited exposure did not gain such a prominent position.

60. This statement is based primarily on my examination of the LISS Study's mailing list.

61. SENE, "How to Guide Growth in Southeastern New England: A Management Proposal for Public Discussion," May 1975. LISS, *Urban Sea*, "People and the Sound: A Plan for Long Island Sound," November 1974.

62. Connecticut River Basin Program, "The River's Reach: A Plan for Flood Damage Reduction and Flood Plain Management in the Connecticut River Basin; 90 Day Public Review Draft," December 1975.

63. LISS, "Report of the Public Workshops of May/June 1973," August 21, 1973, p. 3.

64. Based on interviews with SENE and LISS staff members.

65. In the meeting summaries, the names of the organizations which the speakers were representing were listed; no identifiable minority group organizations were listed.

66. LISS, "Report of May/June Workshops," p. 3.

67. Jenene Geerdes, "Communications Aspects of the Long Island Sound Study," unpublished Master's Thesis, Graduate School of Corporate and Political Communication, Fairfield University, June 1975, pp. 37–39.

68. Ibid., pp. 23–28.

69. See Lester W. Milbrath, *An Extra Dimension of Representation in Water Resources Planning: A Survey Study of Erie and Niagara Counties* (Buffalo, State University of New York, 1976).

4. Participation and the NERBC Plans

1. An earlier version of this chapter first appeared in Madge O. Ertel and Stuart G. Koch, *Citizen Participation in Comprehensive Water Resources Planning* (Amherst, Mass., Water Resources Research Center, University of Massachusetts, August 1976).

2. LISS, "Minutes of CAC Meeting, No. 7," January 10, 1973, p. 2.

3. LISS, CAC, "Goals" (above, p. 170, note 45).

4. LISS, "Minutes of CAC Meeting, no. 19," January 22, 1974.

5. This assessment is based on my interview with the second LISS Manager, David Holmes, September 9, 1975.

6. LISS, "Minutes of CAC Meeting, No. 18," November 27, 1973, pp. 1–2. See also Ertel, p. 85.

7. LISS, "Minutes of CAC Meeting, No. 18," p. 3.

8. NERBC, *People and the Sound: Land Use* (Boston, 1975) and *People and the Sound: Marine Transportation* (Boston, 1975).

9. LISS, "Minutes of CAC Meetings, Nos. 12, 15 and 16."

10. LISS, "Minutes of CAC Meeting, No. 18"; also LISS, Citizen Advisory Committee Memorandum, October 5, 1975.

11. LISS, "Minutes of CAC Meeting, No. 19."

12. LISS, "Minutes of CAC Meeting of June 3, 1974," pp. 1–3.

13. Ibid., p. 3.

14. LISS, "Minutes of CAC Meeting, No. 24," September 18, 1974, p. 8.

15. NERBC, *People and the Sound—Supplement*, pp. 181–203.

16. LISS, "CAC Comments on the LISS Draft Plan," CAC Memorandum No. 75-15, February 25, 1975.

17. Ibid.

18. Ertel, p. 97.

19. NERBC, *People and the Sound—Supplement*, p. 19. See also LISS, "CAC Minutes, No. 19."

20. J. L. McHugh and H. M. Austin, "Prospects for Managing the Fisheries of Long Island Sound," unpublished paper presented at December 1973, R/PAC Seminar, sponsored by LISS.

21. Comments made at R/PAC meeting, January 23, 1974.

22. Comments made at R/PAC meeting, August 6, 1974.

23. LISS, "Report of the Public Workshops of May/June 1973," October 19, 1973.

24. Ibid.

25. LISS, "Results of the Opinion Poll Conducted by the Long Island Sound Regional Study," July 9, 1974.

26. Ibid.

27. LISS, "Selected Newsclips of the Spring 1974 Public Meetings," May 31, 1974.

28. These may be identified by reading the minutes of the various public meetings of January 1975 as prepared by the LISS staff.

29. These issues were categorized by first identifying the issues raised in the minutes of the meetings and then by counting the number of statements both for and against the staff's recommendations. First-hand observation of these meetings assisted in this exercise.

30. The staff summarized in outline form citizen and agency comments and their reaction to them in the last section of the final LISS report, *People and the Sound—Supplement*, pp. 216–220. To assess the accuracy of this summary, I compared the texts of the draft and final reports. See p. 220.

31. Ibid., p. 218.

32. Ibid., p. 219.

33. LISS, "Minutes of New London Public Meeting," January 7, 1975, p. 4.

34. NERBC, *People and the Sound—Supplement*, p. 219.

35. Ibid.

36. Ibid., pp. 216–217.

37. As mentioned above, SENE called for the formation of Basin Advisory Committees (BAC's), but the BAC's consisted of whoever attended the publicly announced meetings. In this report, therefore, what the SENE staff at times called BAC meetings are simply referred to as public meetings.

38. SENE, "Minutes of Meeting No. 5 of CAC and R/STF," March 26, 1973, p. 5.

39. SENE, "Progress Report," p. 2, and an interview with SENE's Public Participation Coordinator, Priscilla Newberry, November 6, 1975.

40. Ibid., p. 4.

41. SENE, "Minutes of Quarterly Meeting of CAC and R/STF," February 11, 1974, pp. 2–4.

42. SENE, CAC, "Goals" (above, p. 170, note 45).

43. SENE, "Minutes of Quarterly Meeting of CAC and R/STF," September 5 and 6, 1974, p. 7.

44. Ibid., pp. 3–10.

45. SENE, "Minutes of Quarterly Meeting of CAC and R/STF," January 3, 1975, p. 6.

46. SENE, "Minutes of Quarterly Meeting of CAC and R/STF," June 24, 1975. See also NERBC, "SENE and the Connecticut River Diversions," Memorandum of July 29, 1975.

47. SENE, "Citizen Preferences for Solutions," sent with a Memorandum to SMT, May 24, 1974; also public announcement to Ipswich–North Shore residents, June 28, 1974.

48. Ibid.

49. SENE, "How to Guide Growth in Southeastern New England: Report of

the Southeastern New England Water and Related Land Resources Study," Review Draft, May 1975. NERBC, *Report of the Southeastern New England Study: Summary, Regional Report (with Environmental Statement), and Ten Planning Area Reports* (Boston, December 1975).

50. Ibid., pp. RR-7.

51. Interview with SENE's Public Participation Coordinator, Priscilla Newberry, November 6, 1975. See also SENE, "Public Meeting Summary; Pawcatuck Planning Area," June 5, 1975, p. 3.

52. SENE, "Public Meeting Summary; Pawtuxet Planning Area," June 4, 1975, pp. 1–2.

53. NERBC, *Report of SENE Study*, pp. RR-4 to RR-5; also SENE, "Public Meeting Summary, Buzzards Bay Planning Area," May 22, 1975.

54. See related articles in *The Chronicle* (weekly newspaper serving North Dartmouth and Westport, Mass.) on July 31, 1975, and August 7 and 14, 1975.

55. NERBC, *Report of SENE Study*, p. RR-7.

56. *Report of the Citizens Review Committee* (above, p. 169, note 15). See also NERBC, *1980 Plan* (above, p. 169, note 16).

57. CRBP, "Report on CAG Meeting of August 11, 1973." Staff members indicated that the original idea of an individual social impact study was presented at an earlier study team meeting by a citizen observer not affiliated with the study.

58. CRBP, "Report on SAG Meeting of March 16, 1973." This is an instance where it is difficult to determine how much credit to give to the advisers (versus the SMT members) for the subsequent action.

59. CRBP, "Memorandum from the SAG Chairman; SAG's Mission and Effectiveness," July 5, 1973.

60. CRBP, "Memorandum," dated August 10, 1973, p. 2.

61. CRBP, "Report on SAG Meeting of July 12, 1973." See also "Report on SAG Meeting of August 23, 1973."

62. CRBP, "Report on SAG Meeting of September 21, 1973," p. 3.

63. For example, CRBP, "Report on SAG Meeting of November 16, 1973," and "Report on SAG Meeting of February 25, 1974."

64. Ibid., and written comments submitted to the CRBP staff and respective agencies.

65. Statements based on interviews with several SAG members and with CRBP staff.

66. CRBP, "Report on Joint CAG and SAG Meeting of October 17, 1974."

67. CRBP, "Report on Joint CAG and SAG Meeting of December 13, 1974."

68. Ibid., and conversations with CAG and SAG members.

69. Ibid., and conversations with CAG and SAG members.

70. CRBP, "Report on Joint CAG and SAG Meeting of May 29, 1975," and interviews with CRBP staff and attendance of this meeting.

71. Ibid.

72. CRBP, "Report on May 1975 Meeting."

73. CRBP, "Report on the Joint CAG and SAG Meeting of July 30, 1975."

74. This was observed by me. I attended the SMT meeting of July 31, 1975.

75. The 90-day public review draft, "The River's Reach: A Plan for Flood Damage Reduction and Flood Plain Management in the Connecticut River Basin," was published by CRBP in December 1975.

76. The comments were compiled in CRBP, "Comments on *The River's*

Reach: 90-day Public Review Draft Report and Environmental Impact Statement," July 1976.
77. NERBC, *The River's Reach: A Unified Program for Flood Plain Management in the Connecticut River Basin* (Boston, December 1976).
78. Ibid., p. 44. Certainly the advisers preferred having both sets of figures
presented rather than just those of the Corps.
79. Ibid., pp. 58, 248.
80. Ibid., pp. 254–55.
81. Ibid., pp. 220–21, 255.
82. CRBP, *Local Perspectives on Flood Management Planning in the Connecticut River Basin; Report on Phase 2 Local Meetings,* November 30, 1974.
83. Ibid.
84. Ibid. See also the final version of NERBC's *River's Reach* (above, note 77).
85. CRBP, *Local Perspectives,* pp. 194–217.
86. CRBP, "The River's Reach; Review Draft," pp. 53–58.
87. CRBP, *Local Perspectives,* p. 132.
88. For a discussion of this rationale, see NERBC's final report, *The River's
Reach,* p. 226.
89. Ibid., p. 249.
90. Ibid., pp. 250–51.
91. Ibid., pp. 252, 253.
92. For further discussion of these points in reference to the LISS Study, see
Robert A. Shanley, *Attitudes and Interactions of Citizen Advisory Groups and
Governmental Officials in the Water Resources Planning Process* (Amherst,
Mass., Water Resources Research Center, University of Massachusetts, August
1976), pp. 60–66.
93. Based on discussions with several advisory committee members; they
clearly viewed the recreational planners as outsiders, unfamiliar with the Long
Island Sound region.

5. Accountability in the NERBC Studies

1. For a similar comment, see Geerdes (above, p. 171, note 67), pp. 33–34.
2. For elaboration on this point see Ertel and Koch (above, p. 171, note 1),
chap. 4.
3. This request was made soon after the CAC began meeting; for more information, see the minutes of these early meetings.
4. LISS, "Minutes of CAC Meetings, No. 12, 15, and 16."
5. For further discussion see Ertel (above, p. 168, note 59), pp. 40–46. See
also CRBP, "Report of the CAG Meeting of July 13, 1973," p. 4.
6. Pitkin (above, p. 161, note 4), chaps. 3–6.
7. This was particularly true with regard to the second CAG Chairman,
Harold Pulling, of Vermont.
8. For a discussion of this point, see NERBC's final version of *The River's
Reach,* pp. 220–21.
9. This point was also made in a letter from CRBP's Study Manager, David
Harrison.
10. Shanley, pp. 46–47, 89.
11. Ertel, pp. 40–46.

12. The CAG Chairman, Mr. Pulling, did report that he had contacted appropriate Vermont officials.

13. Among the advisory committee members included in this category were those appointed by the NERBC Chair, rather than by the respective governors.

14. Ron Nelson, "Level B Water Resources Planning in an Urban Setting," *Water Resources Bulletin*, 11 (1975), 611.

15. Jerry Delli Priscoli, *Public Participation in Regional Level B Water Resources Planning: A Preliminary View* (Washington, D.C., Water Resources Council, Special Consulting Report, October 1974), p. 144.

16. These statements were made by the second LISS Study Manager, David Holmes, in an interview with me on September 11, 1975.

17. Ibid.

18. A comment made by Claire Stein at a LISS public meeting held on January 14, 1975, at C. W. Post College.

19. LISS, Memorandum No. 75-27, from Frank Gregg, Chairman of NERBC, April 11, 1975.

20. The existence of this dual role was acknowledged by Gregg in a conversation with Madge Ertel on October 25, 1973.

21. Delli Priscoli (1974), pp. 79–80.

22. CRBP, *The Local Perspectives Report* (above, p. 174, note 82).

23. The importance of these reports was emphasized by the CRBP Study Manager in an interview with me in June 1976. He saw these as a mechanism for responding systematically to the comments of citizen advisers.

24. For example, see NERBC, *People and the Sound—Supplement*, Section 5.3, pp. 216–21.

25. Delli Priscoli (1974), pp. 81, 91, 120.

26. Ibid., p. 81.

27. Ibid., p. 91.

28. Perhaps the most clear-cut example of such frustrations was a letter of resignation submitted to the CRBP staff from Charles Weaver, who was at the time vice-chairman of the Citizens Advisory Group.

29. Delli Priscoli (1974), pp. 156–57.

30. Citizens did participate in the formulation of the CRBP plan of study, more so than for the other studies.

31. Certain of the recommendations of the Interim CAC's were included in the portion of the plans of study dealing with the public participation programs.

32. Ortolano (above, p. 167, note 54), pp. 3–9, 3–10.

33. Sax (above, p. 164, note 58), p. 102.

34. This question was not asked of the LISS respondents but was subsequently added to the SENE and CRBP questionnaires.

35. Many discussions at the meetings centered on the relocation of structures and possible prohibition of building new structures in flood-prone areas. Property owners also expressed fears that the HUD mapping procedures would diminish the value of those properties identified as being in such areas.

36. From an interview with Priscilla Newberry of the SENE staff, held November 6, 1975.

37. This point was made in a letter from the CRBP Study Manager, David Harrison.

38. Hanchey (above, p. 167, note 54), p. 27.
39. Ibid.
40. NERBC did not systematically keep track of the participation expenses in and of themselves. These rough estimates were provided by Brian Johnson, NERBC's Administrative Officer, who explained that the small percentage of funds involved did not warrant keeping separate records. The expenditures represented about 7 percent of NERBC's own budget for each study.
41. LISS, CAC, "Goals."
42. This is, of course, a difficult distinction to make, but when one examines the instances when the staffs followed citizen advice, one can readily find a number of technical, nonpolitical, reasons for their doing so.
43. Delli Priscoli (1974), p. 179.
44. Ibid.
45. For further discussion see Sharkansky (above, p. 168, note 72), especially chap. 3.
46. Wengert (above, p. 164, note 3), p. 15.
47. From an interview with David Holmes of the LISS staff on September 11, 1975. Delli Priscoli (1974), p. 111, makes the same point.
48. All staff members with whom I discussed this subject emphasized the inadequacy in terms of time to deal with such concerns.
49. Reservations about using the CAC members in such a manner, as discussed by the staff members, centered on the uncertainty of what the citizens would say and the lack of staff control over such situations.
50. Delli Priscoli (1974), p. 165.
51. Ron Nelson, the Public Participation Coordinator of LISS, has noted this particular need; see Nelson (note 14 above), p. 611.
52. Tucker (above, p. 165, note 18), p. 261.
53. Ibid., p. 262.
54. One useful technique used in the CRBP Study was to meet with local and county officials in an afternoon session prior to the public hearing scheduled for that night in the area.
55. LISS, "Minutes of CAC Meeting No. 10," held April 10, 1973. James (above, p. 165, note 14).
56. Shanley, p. 94.
57. From the interview with David Holmes, September 11, 1975.
58. In this case the Water Resources Council and NERBC are jointly handling the Study's funds, although a few agencies, like the Soil Conservation Service, retain some autonomy.
59. David A. Gregorka, *The Citizen Participation Program of the Maumee River Basin Level B Study* (Ann Arbor, Mich., Water Resources Management Program, University of Michigan, 1974), p. 33.
60. Melvin B. Mogulof, *Citizen Participation: The Local Perspective* (Washington, D.C., Urban Institute, March 1970), p. 13.
61. Ertel and Koch (1976), pp. 74–75.
62. Delli Priscoli (1974), pp. 92–93.
63. Ibid., p. 80.
64. The efforts of the CRBP staff, described above, are a step in this direction.
65. The Great Lakes Basin Commission, for example, issues periodically a

newsletter called *The Communicator*. NERBC is the only river basin commission that does not employ this device.

66. Hanchey, p. 25.

6. Participation and Accountability

1. Warner, p. 37.
2. Mogulof, pp. 142, 149.
3. Bishop, p. 108.
4. A level C study is focused on a specific problem and performed prior to the start of construction.
5. Hanchey, p. 34.
6. Derthick, p. 147.
7. League, p. 3.
8. See Sharkansky, chap. 3.
9. Ibid.
10. Derthick, p. 147.
11. See Daniel J. Elazar, *American Federalism: A View from the States* (New York, Thomas Crowell, 1972).
12. Mogulof, p. 161.
13. Hanchey, p. 2.
14. Delli Priscoli (1974), p. 135.
15. Sax, p. 101.
16. Berger, p. 1.
17. National Water Commission, p. 366. In February 1977 a federal judge voided the Government's sale of drilling rights off the Atlantic shore because of deficiencies in the related public hearings and environmental impact statements. See *New York Times*, February 18, 1977, pp. A-1 and B-7.
18. Terence P. Curran, "Water Resources Management in the Public Interest," *Water Resources Bulletin*, 7 (1971), 33–34.
19. National Water Commission, p. 366.
20. Sax, p. 104.
21. Ibid.
22. Delli Priscoli (1974), p. 140.
23. Warner, pp. 9–10. Mogulof, pp. 173–80.
24. Mogulof, p. 61.
25. For further discussion, see Warner, p. 9.
26. These meetings were held in different regions by a private firm under contract to EPA.
27. Ortolano, p. 1–6.
28. Fritschler, p. 4.
29. Among the key members of Congress are the leaders of the Senate and House Public Works Committees.
30. Fritschler, p. 4.
31. For a discussion of the Hoover Commission Task Force, see Ben Moreell, *Our Nation's Water Resources—Policies and Politics* (Chicago, Law School of University of Chicago, 1956).
32. Helen Ingram, "Patterns of Politics in Water Resources Development," *Natural Resources Journal*, 11 (1971), esp. pp. 107–11.

33. Maass, pp. 140–41.
34. Ingram, p. 109.
35. In discussing the failure of the Teton Dam, one observer noted that the project must have involved an "inferior grade of pork"; see Gallagher, p. 108.
36. Ingram, pp. 105, 116.
37. Ibid., p. 117.
38. For a more elaborate discussion of citizens pursuing court action, see Sax.
39. Citizens' Advisory Committee on Environmental Quality, *Report to the President and to the Council on Environmental Quality* (Washington, D.C., December 1975), p. 30.
40. See NERBC, *People and the Sound—Supplement*, pp. 216–21. NERBC, *Report of the SENE Study*, pp. RR-1 to RR-11. NERBC, *The River's Reach*, pp. 241–57.
41. Warner, p. 10.
42. Sax, p. 148.
43. Murphy, pp. 353–55.
44. Ruth Ittner and Dorothee S. Pealy, "Citizen Participation; Search for Criteria," *Washington Public Policy Notes*, Institute of Governmental Research, University of Washington, Seattle, Wash., 5 (1977).
45. See the *Report of the Citizens Review Committee*.
46. This point was made in a letter from the CRBP Study Manager, David Harrison.
47. Thomas Halper, *Foreign Policy Crisis: Appearance and Reality in Decision Making* (Columbus, Ohio, Charles E. Merrill, 1971), chap. 1.
48. Moynihan. Little has been written about participation in the new Community Development programs; yet from my observations, many of these same problems still exist.
49. Woll (above, p. 161, note 6), pp. 18–22.
50. Ibid., p. 248.
51. Wengert, p. 14.
52. Frauenglass, pp. 492–93.
53. Curran, p. 37.
54. Wengert, p. 15.
55. Doerksen and Pierce.

Index

Library of Congress Cataloging in Publication Data

Koch, Stuart G
  Water resources planning in New England.

  Bibliography: p.
  Includes index.
  1. Water resources development—New England—
Planning. I. Title.
TC423.15.K62   333.91′00974   79-66453
ISBN 0-87451-176-3